CAPTURE BY
SOMALI PIk

& other events at sea
1954-2010

COLIN DARCH

Colin Darch

HOLT COTTAGE PRESS

Holt Cottage Press
1 Holt Cottages
Richmond Rd.
Appledore
Devon EX39 1QN

ISBN 978-0-9575931-0-7

Printed and bound by SRP Ltd. Exeter

DEDICATION

To my wife Barbara.
My sheet anchor throughout the storms of life.

ACKNOWLEDGEMENTS

I would like to thank Nigel Dalby for encouraging me to write this book, for designing the front and back covers, and for providing the picture of M.S.Oldenburg on page 59
USNS Carney for providing the front cover picture of "Svitzer Korsakov" anchored off Gabbac, Somalia.
Kieran Tanner for invaluable help in preparing the manuscript for printing.

Contents.

Introduction.

ILLUSTRATIONS

Introduction.

Many seamen of my generation led similar lives to mine, and I felt my life no more worthy of a book than any other. That was until I had the piracy experience which, I felt was unusual enough to warrant recording.

As a first and last book it has not been easy, and I have worried about offending people, and possibly facing litigation. This threatened to inhibit my narrative, so I have changed some names, and written it just as it happened, though seen from my perspective. For the same reason I make no excuse for occasional profanity. It was a man's world in which I lived and the language was often coarse.

Appledore 2013

1:PIRATE ATTACK!

She bucked and reared, plunged and rolled, as I thrashed her stern violently from side to side, with three thousand horse power of thrust in each hand, propeller pitch and revs at maximum. Like a black beast in her death throes the tug crashed through a maelstrom of foam, engines groaning under the strain. In the wheelhouse we shouted and swore in English and Russian, frantic with anger and fear, desperately .fighting to prevent a boarding. Through cascades of white water we had glimpses of two boats of pirates, dark faces, rag heads, and black assault rifles spitting fire, staccato bursts, "crack! crack! crack!" Several times I almost smashed them yet they sheered away and darted in again, recklessly pressing home the attack. Then a shout, "They're aboard!" Defeated, I dropped the revs, with my thumbs reduced propeller pitch to zero thrust, brought the nozzles together, and she stopped dead in the water, which fell calm around us. In the wheelhouse there was silence, while outside pirates clattered up the steel stairways, screaming and shooting in triumph, racing to get at us.

If I thought anything in those few seconds it was probably "How the hell did I get myself into this?" This would be the sternest test of my sea career.

It all began over fifty years before in a North Devon village where I grew up. With my father I moved flags about the maps on our kitchen walls as armies advanced and retreated in World War ll. Food parcels came from relatives in Canada and the United States. A great aunt, in her nineties, told of how she had lived in Japan between the wars, and loved the people. This was in stark contrast to the horror stories we were hearing of Japanese behaviour in China, and Burma, and their treatment of prisoners of war. An uncle flew Sunderland flying boats from Iceland on u-boat patrol, and his brother had emigrated to Australia in the 20's, though contact with him had lapsed. I longed to travel and see the world, and perhaps find that uncle.

I decided the best way to travel would be to go to sea, and be paid for the privilege. Someone advised me to apply for an apprenticeship with a Shipping Company, so I got a list of addresses and wrote letters, earnest and polite. I had five "O" level passes but they did not include Maths, which I discovered for most Companies was essential. Then a seaman advised "Try Reardon Smiths, they'll take anybody!" Although Sir William Reardon Smith came from nearby Appledore in North Devon his offices were in Cardiff, so I wrote there, and was soon signed up for a four year deck apprenticeship, and told to stay at school until they had a ship available. Perhaps inconveniently I was in love with a local girl for most of my last year at home. Before going away I carved our names on a beech tree near a stile on the crest of Buckingham's Hill, from which we could see Exmoor to the east and to the west Lundy Island and the Atlantic, which British seamen call "The Western Ocean." I think of it now as I play "Blueberry Hill" on my saxophone.

2:Indentured Apprentice.

On 27th April 1954 aged sixteen I joined the M.V. "Cornish City, in Falmouth, and signed "Two year Articles," meaning that we could be kept at sea up to two years without leave.
I made my way to Falmouth by train and finally taxi to the ship at Sillely Cox dock preparing for sea. Arrived on deck with my brand new sea-bag shouldered, I was greeted by a Mate, who called a young lad to show me to my cabin. I followed him along the deck thinking what an incredibly filthy individual he was. His long hair merged with a full ginger beard, tangled and unwholesome, and trousers and shirt literally glazed with dirt. "Here, you can have my cabin," said Ginger, "I'm paying off now you've arrived." With that he stripped naked, threw his disgusting togs into a waste bin, dressed in clean "go-ashore" kit and disappeared. Soon I was joined by another first tripper, Dave, and a second year apprentice Reg, and finally the senior apprentice Geoff, aged nineteen and in his last year. Though small, he seemed much older and harder than the rest of us, and was very much in control, laying down strict rules regarding cleanliness in our accommodation, duty rosters for the chores, and making it abundantly clear that he was to be obeyed in all things. When drunk, which was frequent, he turned nasty.

The week or so we lay in Falmouth was a whirlwind of work, ordered about by strange impatient men, and cursed at for being slow and stupid. We loaded tons of stores of all kinds, foodstuffs, including frozen sides of beef, pork, and mutton, coils of rope and wire, drums of paint, bales of canvas, buckets and brooms, bags of rags, sawdust, and cement, all to be stowed in lockers with strange names which had to be located and remembered.

The language of ships was at first quite incomprehensible. The cook was always "doc," the mess-boy "Peggy," and dirty washing "dhoby."
Floors were not floors, and ceilings were not ceilings. To hear my shipmates talk you'd think the ship was a zoo. There were duckboards, catwalks, ratlines, bulldog grips and crocodile clips. Mare's tails in the sky, cats' paws on the sea, and a fishplate round the edge of the deck. Steel doors and hatches were secured by dogs or butterflies. The lifeboat covers had shark's teeth, and on top of the wheelhouse was a monkey island. Heaving lines had a monkey fist at one end and a dog's cock (backsplice) at the other. Up the mast above the crowsnest was a hound's band, and all derricks including the jumbo had goosenecks. To top a derrick one used a bullwire to haul down a monkey face, a triangle plate with three large holes, to shackle to a chain. If the end of a guy travelled along an iron rod it was an iron horse. There were cow hitches, sheepshanks, and mousings. A short rope with an eye at one end was a lizard. Rope yarns for worming, or plaiting into sennit, was made up into

small bundles called foxes. The bilge suctions had rose boxes around them. There were gypsies on the windlass, and a donkeyman to tend the donkey boiler.

Until this jargon was mastered one was conspicuously not a seaman. Fortunately at night we went ashore and drank beer together which helped the process of integration. Tough old men who had cursed you during the day for clumsiness, bought you a beer and said you had worked hard and were learning fast. The money mother had given me soon ran low and I realised I needed more suitable working clothes. The senior apprentice told me to go and ask the Old Man for a "sub," advance of pay, so thinking this no worse than seeing the headmaster I went up to the Captain's cabin and knocked. A hatchet faced character opened the door, glared down at me and barked "What do you want?"
"Please sir can I have a sub to buy some work clothes?" I asked politely.
"Not a penny!" He replied, closing the door.
My first year's wage was £82, which equated to six pounds sixteen shillings and eight pence per month, or 54 pence per day. (in old money.)

At last the ship was ready for sea and we slipped our moorings, left Falmouth harbour, rounded the Lizard, and headed across the "western" for New York. This verse from an old chanty could not have been more appropriate –

"Bold through all or scuppers under, when shall we come back I wonder?
    From the green and chancy water we shall all come back again
To the Lizard and the ladies---but who can say for when?"

But any romantic thoughts were soon banished by the seasickness which overwhelmed me. I had expected it, but the severity and frequency of vomiting day after day alarmed me. There was no sympathy. It was something that had to be endured until the body adjusted to the motion of the ship in a seaway. There was no point lying in a bunk being sick, so one carried on working. The main job was down the empty holds sweeping up the remains of old cargoes to prepare for loading grain in the States.
"Just spew into the pile and keep on sweeping," I was told. "Carry a bread crust in your shirt pocket to chew and give your guts something to throw up," I was advised. And after a particularly spectacular bout of heaving,
"If you feel a gristly ring come into your throat swallow hard, it's your anal sphincter!" Dave my pal was as wretched as me, but the other two benefited from eating our unwanted "whack" of food.

We fetched our food from the galley in a set of kits. These were four shallow pans carried by a handle with extended arms which fitted through rings on the sides of the kits, the top one having a lid. The senior apprentice dished it out. First, soup into four mugs, then the meat or fish onto plates. The third kit contained rice or spuds and vegetables, and the bottom kit "duff". This could be semolina, steamed pudding, or fruit, prunes, or dried apricots always referred to as "Nun's ...." (vulvas). The same plate was used for all courses to save washing up. We were issued a few inches of yellow soap extruded in square section, for general use, scrubbing clothes, tables, pots and pans, and a weekly cake of Japanese toilet soap containing sharp bits of soda, and sometimes there was "Bombay" soap, a softer concoction which came in half coconuts. All scraps of soap went into a tin hanging under the hot tap at the sink, for dish washing.

Tramp ships in those days made about ten knots, (a knot being one nautical mile per hour.) So it took us about thirteen days to roll and plunge our way to Erie Basin, Brooklyn, N.Y. by which time my sea sickness was tolerable. After leaving Brooklyn with a cargo of grain for East London, South Africa, I was not sick and have never been sea sick again. I think it's like swimming or riding a bike, once you get the hang of it you never lose it.

First-trippers in New York, me on the right

The sea routine was pleasant enough. Seamen and apprentices were split into three watches, 12 to 4, 4 to 8, and 8 to 12, three in a watch with any spare hands put on day work, 7am to 5pm with an hour each for breakfast and lunch. Thus all hands worked an 8 hour day, with Saturday afternoon and Sunday off, except for the watch-keepers. The bosun got the day's jobs from the Mate and apportioned the work according to ability. I remarked that one of the A.B.s (Able Bodied Seaman) seemed particularly keen, always first to collect his tools and set to. "He's a headworker," I was told, "working his head." He gets to the job first and choses the best spot, in the shade if hot, in the sun if cold, or perched on top of a winch scraping paint and light rust, but when you arrive you find yourself under the winch chipping the bearers among the congealed oil, filth, and piss. The headworker appears keen but he actually dodges hard work. However, a good Mate and Bosun will recognise the headworkers. Then on a passage where a lot of work has to be done, involving overtime, the headworker will find himself on day work, eight hours work for normal pay. The good men, or favourites, will be on early or late watches, free to earn a lot of overtime during the day.

Reardon Smith's ships, like other tramps, were run on a shoestring. Decks were never painted. We fetched waste oil from the engine room, in old five gallon paint drums, and spread that over the steel decks with mops we made ourselves. Rope yarns were salvaged from old broken ends of rope and plaited into strips of sennit which was seized onto broom handles. The oil lifted the rust whereas paint would simply cover it up. Safety nets and cargo "save-alls" were also made on board from the miles of sennit we made when it was too rough to work on deck. Passing posh ships in port we saw they had purpose-built wind scoops out of their scuttles, (port holes), cone shaped and of a uniform colour. Tramps had five gallon paint drums cut in half lengthways which fitted and served just as well, and were multi coloured. When hold cleaning, anything which could possibly be used again was saved. The rest went over the side into "the big locker."

In East London dozens of black workers, male and female toiled in the holds filling gunny sacks with grain, sewing them up, and then hoisting them out by means of the ship's derricks, and lowering them into railway wagons alongside. This process took three weeks and then we made a two day passage up the coast to Durban, to load coal for Port Sudan in the Red Sea. Our berth in Durban was at the Bluff, near an offshore whaling station which stank to high heaven. A prison on top of the Bluff supplied gangs of prisoners who arrived chained together in trucks. They were then unshackled and spent the day cleaning coal from the tracks on which railway wagons arrived night and day with our coal. A ferry service ran between the Point, near the smart centre of Durban, and the Bluff for crews of ships berthed there. Due, it was said, to strikes at the mines near Jo'burg the cargo of coal took a month to load, and our crew enjoyed plenty of time ashore. One night Geoff, the senior apprentice, and a steward, missed the last ferry back at midnight, so seeing it unattended, started the engine, cast off, and brought themselves home. As nightwatchman I observed this drama unfolding; an erratic launch being tracked by a harbour tug with a searchlight, the gap narrowing steadily, until finally the launch hit the quay and two shadowy figures jumped ashore and disappeared among the coal heaps. Eventually they came aboard, black with coaldust, drunk and laughing, but soon followed by Afrikaaner cops who arrested them. Next day old hatchet face took me with him to the court as a witness, though fortunately I was not asked to speak. Apart from paying for damage to the launch they each received six cuts with a rattan cane. Geoff had me photograph his backside, with spots of blood where the welts crossed, so that his father could sue the South African police, "for assault and battery!"

After discharging in Port Sudan we went further up the Red sea and loaded phosphates at El Quseir, for Japan.

When we finally arrived in Japan I was completely captivated by the country. Just nine years after the devastation of the world war the Japanese were working like demons to restore their prosperity.
Tramp ships were delivering cargo after cargo of raw materials, coal, iron ore, all kinds of minerals and chemicals, rubber, timber, sugar and grain. Wherever else in the world our tramping took us it always brought us sooner or later to Japan, and I loved it. Once away from the docks I found a fascinating world of strange customs, polite people, and a language unrelated to anything else I had ever heard. My love affair with Japan began.

Our wanderings finally led to Western Australia, the port of Fremantle, which the Aussies pronounce Fre'mantle, with the stress on the second syllable as in "disciple." There we loaded grain for Rotterdam.
On sailing day most of the crew including Geoff were ashore in the pubs. As the hour of departure neared they all came back except Geoff. The Third Mate came and told us to remove anything of ours from Geoff's cabin as his effects would be sequestered in the event of him missing the ship. The pilot came aboard, and we made fast a tug to pull us gently away from the quay. Stern ropes were cast off and we began to sheer away when Geoff appeared around a shed staggering towards us. A plank was thrown down for him to step across which he just managed before the plank fell away. Then he picked up a hatch

wedge and shouted that he was going to "fill-in" the Chief Steward. Shortly after that we saw the Steward carrying him over his shoulder to our accommodation where he dumped him in a heap, bleeding from the mouth. Then the Mate arrived with hand cuffs and secured one of Geoff's wrists to a radiator saying he should stay there overnight to sober up. But with his free hand Geoff reached his chipping hammer and after a lot of smashing and cursing he broke the link, and stumbled out on deck, where he finally fell asleep on the hatch.

A six week's trip round the Cape of Good Hope, brought the voyage to an end after eight and a half months. At Rotterdam the crew was paid off and I was sent home by ferry and train to see my family and girlfriend.

"Sweet, Oh! Sweet, is that sensation when two hearts in union meet,
    But the pain of separation mingles bitter with the sweet."

Ten days later the ship called at Falmouth to take fuel bunkers and I was ordered to rejoin. My father drove me down, and we found the crew assembled on a dock waiting to be ferried out to the ship at anchor in Falmouth Roads. The Captain was busy with agents but seeing the Chief Engineer standing alone I took my father over and introduced him. Father asked how I was doing, and the old Geordie replied,
  "Yaw lad's ah reet! He's got what it takes." Praise indeed from an engineer for a deck apprentice.

When we got on board I discovered that the other two apprentices had had their indentures "torn up", cancelled, fired, and the senior apprentice given a D.R. in his discharge book. Decline to Report was the severe criticism permitted in that important document, as the only alternative to Good, or V. G. So I was the only survivor.

The new crew was similar to the previous, drawn from various Shipping Federation pools around the country. There were usually one or two ex Royal Navy men, "matelots," among them, distinguished mainly by their heavy tattooing, acquired during long stays at naval bases such as Gibraltar, Malta, Singapore, and Hong Kong. Merchant seamen had few if any tattoos.

So commenced another spell of world wandering.
  At one point we were anchored at Lataqiya, Syria, unloading grain into barges, after being bagged in the hold and hoisted out in slings. I was awakened one night by the ship's whistle

repeatedly blown. I got up to investigate and the Irish bosun explained. Apparently a worker in the hold had got a foot in the bight of a sling, and when the winchman hauled tight he was dragged under the heavy load of sacks and his foot was torn off. The whistle blasts had been to summon a launch to take the man ashore.

I asked how the poor devil looked.

"Well," said the bosun, "He was alright, shouting at the winchman and hatchman, who caused his injury, and smoking a fag, until some bastard t'rew his foot into the boat, and it hit him in the chest, and he fainted!"

3:Lost Innocence.

Another time we took a load of grain to Rijeka, said to be the birth place of Marco Polo. It was under Tito at the time, and looked pretty grim. Old women with headscarves, men's coats, trousers and heavy boots, swept the gleanings from the quay with witches brooms. I was nightwatchman, and helped the crew back aboard as they arrived in dribs and drabs from good times ashore. They said despite the overall greyness and poverty of this communist country there was a thriving night life. Booze and women were cheap. I decided to sample some of this, and turned some sterling into dinars, sold a couple of woollen jumpers, and arranged another apprentice to do my Saturday night duty. Before turning in on Saturday morning I went to the galley for my breakfast, and was alarmed to hear the doc say we would be sailing that afternoon or early evening. And there was I with about £4 of dinars to spend, useless in any other country. The only thing to do would be to go ashore that morning and try to buy presents or souvenirs for my family and girlfriend. Hearing this the cook asked me to do him a favour. He had had the same girl for a week, and asked me to take her his apologies, for not being able to see her again. He sketched directions to her house, and explained that it was a French speaking Belgian family, and the mother operated a brothel with several of her daughters. I was proud of my "O" level French and readily agreed to the errand; always wise to get on the right side of the doc. In blazer and slacks I went ashore and found the stone steps leading up to "mamasan's" door, at which I knocked. A stout lady appeared and in my carefully rehearsed French I passed the message. She thanked me and promised to pass it on to her daughter, so I left and went shopping. Alas, I found nothing at all worth buying, so had a beer or two and got to thinking. The result was that I went back up the stone stairs and knocked at the door again. The old mother gave me a quizzical look as I urbanely enquired whether, as I was at a loose end, she could point me in the direction of a girl. At this she laughed and called over her shoulder to one of her daughters. They studied me, the young man of the world, while they laughed and babbled away in rapid French, completely beyond my comprehension until the name "Genevieve" emerged. Then I followed mother down a passage to a door which opened into a sort of dormitory with several beds. One girl was asleep in a far corner and Genevieve's bed was just behind the door. The girl was clearly disgusted to be told she had a "client," at 1030 in the morning, and asked for a cigarette. While she smoked and shot me hostile glances I shyly undressed and got into bed beside her. She finished the cigarette, stubbed it out, and lay back for me to do the business. But I was awkward and clumsy and blurted out, "C'est le premier fois pour moi." This changed her mood completely. She stared at me incredulously, before dissolving into noisy laughter. To add to my confusion her mother suddenly opened the door and entered with two glasses of schnapps. It tasted like sulphuric acid. After that I was initiated into the joys of sex. Then I dressed and without asking the price put all the money I had, about three weeks' wages, on her bedside table. Some say virgins get it free, but that only applies to girls. I walked back to the ship with a contented smile. I had brought so much laughter to that household.

That evening, at sea, one of the older seamen, a "sea daddy," explained to me the dangers of promiscuous sex. He said if I had the usual problem the unmistakable symptoms would appear between two and nine days, in the form of peeing razor blades or broken bottles. When I asked what would happen if I did have the unfortunate problem, I was told that the Old Man had the wherewithal to cure me, by bending me over and sticking a hypodermic needle in my bum with antibiotics. After an anxious nine days I was presumed clear.

From Yugoslavia we went through the Suez Canal down to Aden to load salt for Japan.
  The salt would all go into hatches one, two, four, and five, missing out number three, the deep tank hatch. So the Mate decided the frames in the tween deck of number three hatch needed strengthening, or hiding, with cement boxes at the base where they had partly rusted away. The carpenter was ordered to build wooden "boxes," or shuttering the whole length of the hatch, port and starboard. The Mate then requisitioned three tons of cement and about ten tons of sand for me, and me alone, to mix and shovel in to fill the boxes. In the open hatch, in the blazing sun, sheltered from any breeze day after day, this was hard work and utterly draining. Every evening I went ashore to the bar of the Crescent Hotel to swallow gallons of cold beer to supply the next day's sweat. And there was the Mate, in a cane chair on the terrace, downing glass after glass of gin and tonic with copious ice. There was a connection. Ordering an expensive item like cement from the ship chandler would have resulted in a nice little commission, or kick-back from chandler to Mate, to finance his gin. Did the job really need doing? Who knows?

While there our Third Mate discovered he had a friend in the R.A.F. camp at Little Aden. He had joined as a newly qualified dentist, and offered free service to 3/O or any shipmates, presumably for practice. I had a spot of decay between my two front rabbit teeth and gladly accepted the offer. He drilled and drilled, and finally announced that one of the teeth would have to come out. As the service was free I couldn't complain.

As the months rolled by and my seamanship improved I began to see this as a possible career instead of just a means of travelling and seeing the world, but for the present my main problem was getting enough to eat. We young apprentices were always hungry. The Board of Trade food allowances were laid out in a large document pinned up in the ship for all to see. But studying it was confusing and unrewarding, as so many alternatives and substitutes were allowed. One just had to trust the Chief Steward would give you your "whack."

"One egg per man per day, except Christmas Day and New Year's Day when he may have two, an' that's yer whack!" For the poor quality the steward blamed the cook, and the cook blamed the steward for supplying him with second rate goods. It was an evil axis.

Meanwhile nothing that came into our messroom was ever wasted, with the sole exception of the so-called "Board of Trade jam." We had a monthly issue of a half gallon tin, with no adornment other than a small white label bearing the B.O.T. badge, and the terse inscription, "Fit for consumption by merchant seamen." From this we inferred that the contents had not quite measured up to normal human food standards, but was too good for animals. The labels also bore a stencilled indication of the colour of the contents, green, yellow, or red. One I remember was "Greengage," (or guage), but otherwise the exact wording escapes me. It might have been "Yellowhammer" and "Red Robin" for what difference it made. They all had the same bland taste with no seeds or skin, a slightly gelatinous texture, and smell. This was a sort of metallic, or chemical odour, not redolent of fruit. Nor was it particularly sticky stuff, and sugar-loving insects such as wasps and cockroaches more or less ignored it. This puzzled us, particularly the indifference of the 'roaches, and gave rise to much speculation. Someone said the constituents were mainly swede, and artificial colourants. Another went further and said it wasn't food at all, but a sort of petroleum jelly intended for the treatment of burns. The theory developed that through a mix up in the factory, these small drums in their thousands had been run through the wrong labelling rollers. Perhaps they actually contained solvents or something, colour coded for different applications in the plastics or textile industries. In the saloon amidships they had different jam in glass jars with pretty labels.

In the end we decided this Board of Trade "jam" had no nutritional value, and was probably not safe to eat. When a few cans accumulated we bartered them away to natives in bum-boats, for bananas and dirty books.

Eventually, after our customary spell in Japan we were ordered across the North Pacific, in winter, to Prince Rupert north of Vancouver. This was a rough, cold, foggy passage, taking us on a "great circle" course up close to the Aleutions. Due to the long dark nights and foggy days a look-out was maintained almost constantly on the fo'c'sle head. The seamen had only one decent heavy coat among them, having sold most of their winter woollies in Yugoslavia, to finance their debauchery. That coat spent many days and nights on the fo'c'sle, with the lookouts handing it over in turn to their reliefs.

Prince Rupert was the central topic of our conversation and speculation for the four weeks before we got there as no-one knew anything about the place. It was a small port set among strong smelling pine forests with characters out of Robert Service poems, and plenty of rather sad looking Indians, of the Siwash tribe I was told. The rough bars had partitions down them from floor to ceiling and reaching right to the bar, to keep men and women segregated. At the bar you could hear them, and even catch a glimpse in the mirror behind the barman, but that was all. After a week or so we sailed for Belfast via the Panama Canal, a long voyage of about six weeks, during which Prince Rupert still figured largely in our conversation. At Belfast I happened to be at the wheel when the pilot came aboard, and among the usual pleasantries he asked where we were from.

"Prince Rupert," replied the Master.

"B' jaysus! Where in hell is that?" He shouted, but didn't listen for any explanation. I thought that just about sums up our tramp ship life. Away for months on end, hither and thither to unheard of places, working, living, suffering, alone and largely forgotten by the normal run of humanity.

I had joined that old ship in April 1954 and it was now January 1956, twenty one months with only ten days at home, so it was time to leave her. But I could not face my beautiful girlfriend with an ugly gap in my front teeth, so I stopped off at Southampton, checked in to a B.& B. near the station, and found a dentist. Several days later, with smile complete, I had my last breakfast and paid the landlady, who was sobbing. When asked why, she said her budgie had died, and pointed to a ball of fluff in the bottom of its cage. I gave her an extra half-a-crown to buy a new one. She was delighted and asked,

"What's your name dearie? I'll call it after you." So there is a budgerigar in Southampton called Colin.

After a couple of glorious months at home I joined the next ship, the "Queen City," in which I spent eleven months. The Captain, Chief Mate, D.L.G.Jones, (David Lloyd George), and Chief Steward, were all Welsh speakers, which made it difficult to complain about the food, they being something of a clique. The same mean Reardon Smith attitude pervaded the ship. I later met an old bosun who had sailed with that skipper when he was Mate. He told me when they were homeward bound up the Channel the Mate announced he was auctioning old clothes, and pinned up a list, which included "two pairs of socks,(one with holes.)"

One day, around Christmas, I was working in the fo'c'sle head sewing canvas with the Bengali cassab. We worked in silence until he looked up with an engaging smile and asked,

"Sahib, what mean Chris'mas?" Though uneducated he had an intelligent look, and I took care with my answer. I explained that Christians believe that around two thousand years ago God sent an angel called Gabriel to earth to plant seed in the womb of the virgin wife of a carpenter called Yussuf, and in December Christians celebrate the anniversary of the birth of this "son of God." The cassab stared at me in complete incredulity, and then burst into laughter and spluttered out,

"Allah he God! He no wife, he no can have chil'!" I felt indignant at first, but then foolish. I had to admit that I had been fed the nativity story since childhood and accepted it without thinking, whereas no rational man hearing it for the first time in middle age could be expected to believe it. It really set me thinking, especially about how Yussuf's wife could be a virgin, surely a contradiction in terms.

Sometime later we loaded grain in Western Australia for Europe and headed for the Cape of Good Hope, alternatively known as the Cape of Storms. The Agulhas Current runs strongly down the African coast and when it is opposed by strong seasonal winds a tremendous sea builds up. We were working our way through this treacherous region when the old "Queen" dug her shoulder into a swell and shipped a green sea. It picked up the little cassab and carried him down the fore deck until slamming him against some steel mooring bitts where he clung until the sea drained away and a couple of men rescued him. His extremities, head hands and feet, appeared unharmed but he was in great pain from the body. The Old Man couldn't decide whether he had a broken pelvis, back, or ribs, so headed for Cape Town. Off Cape Town we rendezvoused with a launch and I was sent ashore with the patient for moral support, and to explain to the doctor how the injuries had occurred. Our agent met us at the dock with an ambulance and we proceeded to the Christian hospital. But there, due to apartheid we were segregated according to colour. I was channelled one way being white, and the Bengali adjudged "coloured" was sent another way and I never saw him again. A report for the Captain was given me in a sealed envelope, and I was returned to the ship. Christianity could not have left a good impression on our little Muslim shipmate.

4: Suddenly an Officer.

At home after that ship I had a shock. Aged nineteen, with a year left to do of my apprenticeship I was ordered to go back to my old ship, the "Cornish City," as Acting Third Mate. Suddenly I was an officer.

It was common practice in those ships to use final year apprentices as Third Mate, uncertificated, with less pay than a properly qualified man. But I was utterly unprepared for the task as I had seldom been on the bridge, except to take my turn at steering in and out of port. At sea the ship was under control of the "iron Mike," automatic helmsman, which steered straighter than a man and therefore saved fuel. So with serious misgivings I joined her in Manchester. It was good to be back in the old tub and to my immense relief I found the Second Mate, John Williams, was from Appledore, near my home, and he assured me he would teach me all I needed to know. He was an excellent teacher, patient and thorough, but I was starting from scratch. Over the coming weeks and months after doing my own 8 to 12 watch I spent a lot of time on John's watch, 12 to 4 learning to take compass bearings, azimuths and amplitudes to check compass error, sights of the sun and moon with the Captain's sextant, the Morse code to signal with an Aldis lamp, basic meteorology, and a lot of other stuff necessary for a watch-keeping officer, not to mention the anti collision rules. I was very keen to learn and worked hard at it. John Williams ultimately passed his Extra Master's Certificate and became a senior lecturer at Southampton University School of Navigation, and has remained a close friend.

Our first port of call was Norfolk, Virginia, to load coal for Japan. The passage to Panama Canal took about a week and then it was thirty five days to Kawasaki in Japan. On the chart Panama was down the right hand side and Japan in the top left hand corner. Our daily progress measured an inch, and there was no land to see along the way. One could easily imagine there was no more land, and no more people.

Eventually we arrived at our berth in Kawasaki and hundreds of Japanese coolies came aboard to shovel the coal into tubs for hoisting ashore. This furious work continued night and day, and it rained most of the time, which combined with the coal dust, and dim glow cast by the ship's cluster-lights, and the steam escaping from the winches as they hammered round, hoisting and lowering, created a scene like Dante's inferno. Then suddenly it all stopped as the lights went out and the winches fell silent. I was the duty officer upon whom the Japanese foremen descended demanding restoration of the power. With a torch I located the Junior Engineer on duty, all others having gone ashore. But he could not start the generator which had failed, or the spare generator. I guess the Japanese were on piece work and their impatience and frustration rose to fury. At last I explained that I would have to go ashore and find another engineer. I knew there was a row of girlie bars just outside the dock gates, and I felt sure an engineer could be found there philandering after so many weeks at sea. They thrust a bicycle into my hands and off I went along the quay through the driving rain. Then disaster struck! The front wheel fell into a railway track which went off at an angle while I pitched straight ahead, skidding on face and hands through the gritty coal. I picked myself up and found the front wheel buckled but the bike still rideable, so I continued on my way. To my great relief I found the Chief Engineer in the very first bar I entered. They were all shocked at my appearance, black with coal, soaking wet, and bleeding from face and hands. When I explained the problem the Chief grabbed a taxi back to the ship, shouting,

"Give the boy a beer!"

Then I was transported into a kind of Japanese paradise. Girls stripped me and took away my clothes to iron dry, and then with bowls of warm soapy water and cotton wool dabbed ever so gently at my wounded face and hands, clucking and cooing affectionately. Actually I insisted on keeping one hand free to drink the cold beers which were charged to the Chief's account. This blissful interlude was eventually terminated by the return of the Chief Engineer. I pushed the bike back to the ship which I found a blaze of lights and the infernal work in full swing. Next morning the Captain complimented me on my initiative.

As I was now "amidships" I had little to do with the apprentices, but one story did filter through.

A curly-headed junior apprentice hurrying back from ashore caught up with the Chief Steward, waddling along with a belly full of booze.

"Slow down, and walk with me," said he, "How are you enjoying the sea life?" The boy said he liked it well enough but was always hungry. The Steward expressed disbelief but invited him to his cabin where he would see what he could find.

He first poured two tumblers of scotch and then went to the pantry from where he returned with half a cold chicken. But first they had to drink the whisky and the Steward became amorous. In panic the young lad said he really should share the chicken with his mates, swallowed the scotch and bolted out the door. His pals were delighted, until one cynical fellow asked what he'd had to do for it.

"Well I allowed him one smoochy kiss on the lips," the boy confessed.

"Get out! And wash your mouth, you disgusting little bastard!" was the angry response, but they all took a share of his half chicken.

One feature of life at sea in those days was the steady arrival of "Dear John" letters. In that ship it became the custom for the sad recipient to pin his "Dear John" to the outside of his door for passers –by to see. The man's name at the top might be John, or Tom, Dick, or Harry, and the girl's at the end could be Mary, Margaret, Delilah, or whatever, but the narrative was always remarkably similar.

"I was so sad and lonely when you left. Then I met this chap who made me laugh, and was kind and considerate, like you. I'm sure you would like him. Well I have fallen in love with him. I'm sure you will find happiness with someone else. I hope we can always be friends."

I decided to be very noble and release my girlfriend from any obligation to me. We had spent so little time together, and she was young and beautiful and should be out enjoying herself. Was this being noble? Or was it that I dreaded a "Dear John " from her and made a sort of pre-emptive strike? To impress my mates I threw all her photographs over the side, except two.

John Williams convinced me that I was capable of passing my Second Mate's Certificate, and progressing in a career at sea, if I wished. After much serious deliberation I concluded that the life suited me well enough, but not in tramp ships with white crews, and belly-robbing stewards. I was sick and tired of all the boozing and fighting that took place as they worked their way through the four stages of drunkenness,-- Jocose, Bellicose, Lachrymose, and Comatose.

  Of all the countries I had visited I preferred Japan, so I enquired about Shipping Companies which specialised in that area. The China Navigation Company, of Butterfield & Swire, Hong Kong seemed ideal. Then by chance in a Yokohama bar I met some officers of the C.N.Co. ship "Chekiang" on her maiden voyage, and they invited me aboard. She was a revelation. I had no idea ships could be so clean and efficient, with Chinese in uniform swarming around doing all the work. After gin and tonics with ice and lemon delivered by a smiling steward, I was invited to stay for lunch. In Reardon Smith's deck officers sat at one long table in a strict pecking order with the Master at the head, while engineers ranged down another table headed by the Chief. There was no banter between the two tables, "oil and water don't mix!" But the saloon in the "Chekiang" had several small round tables, where anyone was free to take any vacant seat. And the food, selected from printed menus, was out of this world. I left that vessel very excited and determined to pass my "ticket" and join the enchanted world of the China Navigation Company.

After an eleven month trip as Third Mate I left the "Cornish City." Of my four year apprenticeship I had spent almost three years in her, and I looked back at her with some affection. There is never another quite like ones first ship, and in her I had grown from a boy to a young man.

M.V. "Cornish City."

M.V."Cornish City," built 1943 by Doxfords of Sunderland as the "Empire Cheer," for the Ministry of War Transport, under Reardon Smith management. 1946 Handed over to Reardon Smith Line and renamed "Cornish City." December 1962 en route from Baton Rouge to Calcutta damaged by engine room explosion and fire at Aden which killed Second Engineer Dougie Chattan, and another. 1963 towed to Hong Kong and broken up.

Left to right Wilfie Evans Fifth Engineer, me Third Mate, Sidney Jewell Fourth Engineer, and John Williams Second Mate. The crew used to group us together being North Devonians, but the other three from Appledore were appalled at this.

 "Don't class ee with us, e's from miles inland! (eleven actually) How he ever came to go to sea us will never know! He can't even scull a boat!" (propel a boat with one oar over the stern.)

Sidney reminded me recently how during that trip we had a serious engine breakdown in the Red Sea, and stopped for several hours to change a piston. Taking a break from his turn in the crank case which was 120 degrees F. he was slumped on number four hatch dripping sweat when the Old Man chanced along.

"I'll bet you would love a cold beer Mr. Jewell," said the Captain, "I'll get you one." The delicious bottle of beer arrived glistening with condensation, and was gratefully received. But Sidney noticed at the end of the month he had been charged for it.

John Williams and I shared digs at Plymouth where we studied at the Plymouth Polytechnic College, me for Second Mate's and him for First Mate's Certificates.

Half my class were from rough and hungry ships like mine, and half from posh companies where the Apprentices, or Cadets, as some were called, had been properly taught and prepared for life as officers. The latter wore smart blazers and ties with company badges, crests with Latin mottoes, and received "study leave pay" while at College. We of the lower order queued for "dole," to which we were entitled as we had no other income. Our funnel markings, "S" for "Starvation Smiths," "H" for "Hungry Hain's" and Tatems," T on the funnel and f'all on the table," and so on, did not lend themselves to blazer badges.

I failed my first attempt at examination through a poor maths paper, but after several months did finally succeed. On the plus side I played a full season of rugby for South Molton, a local market town.

5: The China Navigation Company.

With my brand new Second Mate's Certificate I went to London, and was interviewed and accepted by the China Navigation Company, at their Dickensian offices in Billiter Square. As their ships did not come to Europe officers were flown out to Hong Kong for a four year tour of duty. I flew in a Qantas Super Constellation as far as Calcutta, where I had a six hour wait in the Great Eastern Hotel, and enjoyed beer, curry, and a bath. Then I continued to Hong Kong in a DC6 of Cathay Pacific Airways, a part of the Swire Group which owned C.N.Co. The whole trip, London to Hong Kong took four calendar days.

In H.K. I was accommodated in the Company's "bungalow" at Quarry Bay, while I got fitted out for sea. Various uniforms, summer and winter, were made for me by Ku Cheong who remained my tailor for eleven years, and shoes, white and black, by shoemaker Lee Kee. I opened an account at the Hong Kong & Shanghai Bank into which my wages would be paid, and got to know a number of other officers of the Company doing "bungalow time," and around the bars and night clubs of Wanchai. All spoke well of the Company which was very encouraging and a contrast to where I had come from. One of my early acquaintances was a Chief Engineer Archie Blue, who had been pirated in the "Nanchang," in 1933 and held for several months in difficult circumstances. I later bought the book, "The Piracy of the Nanchang."

My first ship, "Anking," instead of trading to Japan, was chartered, together with "Anshun," to shuttle "Hadjis," Muslim pilgrims, from Singapore and Penang to Jiddah, the port for the holy cities of Meccah and Medina.

The "Anking" carried over eleven hundred pilgrims per trip from Singapore and Penang, leaving them at Jiddah and returning to Malaysia for more until the three special holy days in July, after which we carried them back again. The whole programme lasted eight months. The hadjis slept on "bally-ballys," tubular metal beds with a sheet of plywood, ranged edge to edge in the tween decks, of which most holds had two, upper and lower. Every day the pilgrims were sent up on deck, section by section, for the Chinese crew to hose down the decks removing vomit, fruit skins, and other rubbish. Signposts were adjusted daily to indicate the direction of Meccah, to which they prayed five times. We carried two Muslim doctors from Pakistan, and two or three Malayan officials to deal with any problems and act as interpreters. On the outward trips almost nobody died, but on the return voyages, having spent several months in the hostile climate of Arabia, and having fulfilled their obligation to visit the holy places, those who went sick or had accidents in rough weather seemed to give up and die without a struggle. We carried a supply of iron fire bars and shrouds to consign them to the deep. We stopped the ship, waited respectfully for a short Muslim service, and then tipped the bodies into the sea. I grew to respect the sincerity and humuility of the pilgrims, and read an English copy of the Koran, without accepting the tenets of Islam. When a young woman had a miscarriage the doctor showed me the three or four month foetus in a jar of formaldehyde, which he was taking back to his university.

Officers of the " Anking," me at right of picture.

During the period between the last outward trip and the first homeward one the pilgrim ships were sent up to Port Tewfik, at the southern end of the Suez Canal, to wait at anchor. I went with other officers to Cairo for a long weekend. We saw the usual sights; pyramids, Mohammad Ali mosque, Cairo museum with the mummies, ex king Farook's palace, and Cairo zoo. When we piled out of a mini-bus at the gates of the zoo we were confronted by a collection of beggars. I was particularly shocked to see a young mother with a naked boy across her knees, apparently dead. He was perfectly still with flies crawling in and out of his open mouth and staring eyes. I dropped some coins in her tin and hurried through the gates, but the image stayed with me all day until we left. Then I saw the boy kicking a ball about with his mates. Later I read that Arabs tolerate flies walking over their flesh, and don't try to brush them away. It was something Lawrence, "of Arabia," had to learn when operating in disguise.

After the pilgrim season "Anking" resumed her normal trading between Hong Kong, Australia, and Japan. I began to study the Japanese language, and to my delight I was appointed Third Mate of the "Chekiang."

She was engaged in the island trade through New Guinea, the Solomons, New Hebrides, Fiji, Samoa and Tahiti. In most ports the Captain berthed his ship without benefit of pilots or boatmen. Early one morning in Kavieng, New Ireland, we approached the little wooden jetty. Starboard side berthing would have been easier but leaving would have been quite difficult. So it was normal to approach with some speed, and drop the starboard anchor to act as a drag and a brake to turn the ship and present her port side to the berth On this particular morning the Old Man misjudged it and we ended up inside the line of the jetty, and the wind blew us onto the coral. The poor Captain was close to tears, lamenting that the nearest tug would be in Brisbane, hundreds of miles away, and his forty year career had come to a shameful end. But here the Mate stepped up. Jim Lough, a dour Scot who had served his time with Salvesens of Leith, Britain's last whalers. He first insisted we all had breakfast while considering what to do. Over breakfast he outlined the plan, which, succeed or fail would impress the underwriters. He would rig a guntackle on one of the forward derricks, break out the spare bower anchor and suspend it over the bow on the ship's "insurance" wire, a heavy wire reserved for towing in emergency. Meanwhile I was to get the two lifeboats over the side, bring them together, secure long awning spars from the boatdeck across the four gunwales, and prepare rope to hang the anchor between the boats. I was proud to be given this important work while my senior, the Second Mate, was assigned to keeping a notebook detailing weather and tide conditions, and recording everything we did for the insurance assessors. This Second Mate liked to wear a blazer with cravat and floppy handkerchief while describing tennis parties with Cynthia, the Lord Lieutenant of Glamorgan's daughter.

While these preparations were going on the Captain received a visit from John Johnstone, a diver who had famously recovered gold from the "Niagara," and was now in Kavieng advising a Japanese diving team inspecting war time wrecks. Johnstone and the Old Man recognised each other as freemasons and Johnstone volunteered to dive and check our propeller and rudder for damage. His report that two prop blades were just slightly distorted was good, and only caused vibration at certain critical revolutions which we could avoid.

The plan worked well. I positioned the boats under the derrick, got the anchor secured in place, and with a chain stopper paid out bights of the wire while Jim revved the motor lifeboat engine and steered us out to a position off the starboard bow. With all wire out, and drifting out of position Jim leapt from the tiller, with two heavy blows of an axe cut the lashing rope, the anchor plunged to the bottom, and the two boats danced crazily in the morning sunshine. We then returned to the ship, bent the heavy wire round the windlass drum end and heaved. To everyone's immense relief we slowly hauled clear of the coral and the Captain calmly put her alongside, his confidence fully restored. We were then invited to large tots of rum with the Captain, and an interesting chat with "Johnno the Deep Sea Diver," (the title of his biography.) The "Niagara" had left Auckland in 1940 bound for Vancouver with roughly half of New Zealand's small arms stock, and eight tons of gold bullion for Britain to buy United States war material. She hit a German mine just north of Auckland and, although all passengers and crew got off she sank in 60 fathoms with all the gold. During 1941 a team, with lead diver Johnstone recovered 555 bars of gold, and in 1953 he returned and his team recovered another 30 bars, leaving only five unaccounted for.

Soon after this I was promoted to Second Mate.

It was the Company's policy to move officers around the ships to widen our experience, so I spent a few months in "Kwangtung," and "Hunan," a delightful old steamer built in 1931. Then, as I had sufficient sea-time to sit for my First Mate's Certificate I went ashore in Hong Kong to study at the Hung Hom Technical College. There was a handful of us Europeans from C.N.Co., and Jardine Mathieson, but the vast majority of students were Chinese. Lunch in the canteen was a bedlam of slurpings, spittings, flashing chopsticks, and oily odours, but at a dollar a dish of chow fan or chow mien we had no complaints.

When I passed that exam I booked a telephone call to my parents to give them the good news. In those days you booked one day for a call the next, from the Cable & Wireless office. The telephone Company also warned the receivers to expect an overseas call. It was mid-morning in England when I got through, and I was amazed to hear how many from our village had packed themselves into our small kitchen for this unprecedented event, a call from the Far East!

For the three months in Hong Kong studying I had a regular girl, a Shanghainese called "Katie." She was a lot older than me, but I liked her, and I knew I could depend on her being in Albert Woo's key club when I wanted her. The official designation of the key club was "H.K. Calligraphy, Literature, and Fine Arts Amateur Friendly Association," but actually it was an all night drinking den. One night as I let myself into the Club I clearly saw Katie turn from seeing me to announce to her friends that "Wah Sung," had arrived. We all knew that we had nicknames, because the Chinese found our western names hard to remember, but, probably because they were derogatory, we rarely got to know them. In this case she was caught, and I persuaded her to divulge the meaning of Wah Sung. She shyly confessed that they called me "Little monkey," because I was inclined to bob about from place to place to talk to various friends, with my hands on the furniture, and never really standing up, like a perambulating ape.

If not at the Key Club I could find her in her tenement apartment. After first locating the sign of the Peacock Laundry I ducked under it, through a doorless entrance and mounted narrow stairs with landings at each floor. On her floor I had to speak her Chinese name several times through a peep hole in a bolted door until someone, usually a child, came and let me in. Beyond the door was a warren of small rooms leading to Katie's three, a kitchen, bedroom, and washroom. One day she related a sad tale. She had seen a young woman on a balcony close by weeping and rocking on her haunches all day. Katie had wondered about the problem and every time she looked the woman was there in obvious distress until, "About five o'clock she jump off!" Then Katie laughed and said, "She clazy."

About this time in a quiet Japanese bar not frequented by foreigners, I met a young girl of thirteen or fourteen who was very keen to learn English. Her parents owned the bar and allowed her to come down and talk to me as long as I was well behaved. Noriko and I found this arrangement mutually beneficial. She got me grammar books, and childrens' story books in "roma-ji," that is to say A,B,C, and my Japanese increased in leaps and bounds, as did her English. I continued to see her until she was twenty one and launched in a career with an American company.

Meanwhile I was enjoying the various parts of the Company's far flung trading empire. Their ships took me to all parts of the China Sea, China, Korea, The Philippines, Malaysia, Indonesia including the Celebes, and on to New Guinea, the Solomons, Fiji, Samoa, and Tahiti. I particularly liked the little out-of-the-way places like Gorontalo, Tilimuta, Papajato, "where bells of Christians never rang." In those sleepy backwaters we loaded copra, coffee beans, trochus shells, sacks of animal bones, and hardwood logs, always for Japan. The pace of life was slow, and the few Europeans encountered were like characters from Joseph Conrad. I remember one Public School type who lived alone with his natives running a copra plantation, and very rarely came into "town." I asked him how near was the next European. His reply,

"Forty miles down the coast, Dutchman, don't like the man."

In the early sixties the president of Indonesia was Soekarno, who was obsessed with the idea of "liberating" the western half of New Guinea, referred to as Irian Barat, and annexing it to Indonesia. The natives of New Guinea were not at all keen to come under the control of Javanese, of a different race and religion, but they had little power of resistance. Soekarno diverted all economic resources to this project and everything else was neglected. In the port of Surabaya a set of cranes which normally ran up and down the quays gradually became immobilised through unloading cargoes underfoot, and as far as they could reach, as high as they could manage, until they were completely stowed in. Nothing was ever removed. Flour in sacks and other perishables rotted and were consumed by rats, while thieves looted boxes and bales. The people were exhorted to endure shortages in the patriotic struggle for Merdeka, for Irian Barat. In this crazy situation with the men away on war duty women were reduced to selling their bodies to feed their children. As this practice becomes more widespread the price falls. We were able to buy Indonesian rupiahs in Singapore at $1 for Rh.100, when a Singapore dollar cost three shillings and fourpence sterling. A woman in Tanjong Priok cost 100 Rupiahs for the night i.e. three and fourpence, or six nights for a pound.

On one occasion a couple of us went up to Bogor, a hill resort above Djakarta, formerly Batavia, the capital of Java. At Bogor there are beautiful botanical gardens created by Lady Raffles, wife of Sir Stamford Raffles, Lieutenant-Governor of Java before he established the settlement at Singapore.

As we strolled through the gardens, a spindly little man in grubby shorts and vest fell into step with us. Thinking him a beggar we ignored him at first, but then realised he was quietly telling us the names, in English and Latin, of all the trees, shrubs, and flowers. Intrigued, we questioned him and heard that, as a boy, he had worked in the gardens, and from the Dutch head gardener had learned the names of everything in Dutch and Latin. Then, when the Japanese over-ran the country and the Dutch were thrown out, he worked for the new masters. He supplied the officers with herbs, spices, and vegetables from the extensive kitchen garden, and learned to name everything in Japanese. Finally, when the Japanese were kicked out at the end of the war, he learned it all again in English, to guide the tourists. We enjoyed his entertainment and tipped him well. He had spent his entire life in those botanical gardens and probably slept in a potting shed, or a pineapple bush. He was a good example of how not to judge a book by its cover.

6:Jungle at night.

The port of Lae lies at the head of the Huon Gulf in New Guinea where the Markham river enters the sea. Lae had only one berth for ships and if you had to wait for this berth the anchorage was on a spit of sand extending from the shore three miles south of the port. We once lay there for several days and the Old Man grew impatient. On a Sunday he announced that on the morrow he would take the motor lifeboat up to the port and stir things up a bit, berate the agent and stevedore, and take lunch at the Club. So Sunday afternoon the Second Engineer, Third Mate, and one seaman took the boat away for a spin to test the engine. As darkness fell we saw the boat nestled in close to the trees where the mangroves of the river delta gave way to jungle. Late that evening the Second Engineer appeared with a native in a dugout canoe he had commandeered to bring him back. He explained that while they had gone exploring the boat had rocked itself into a pit, and the three of them could not dislodge her. The Mate sent me and three seamen in our small workboat, rowing ashore with sandwiches and whisky to rescue our lifeboat and shipmates. It was a pitch black night with heavy tropical showers, and our combined efforts still failed to get the heavy boat afloat. I decided to send everyone back in the workboat, while I spent the night protecting the lifeboat from being plundered by natives who had probably noticed her vulnerable position. Off they went into the darkness and I settled down with an oil lamp and the whisky for company. The lamp attracted swarms of mosquitoes, and the rain drenched and chilled me, while red and white "eyes" of glow worms and fireflies winked at me from above. The jungle at night is full of hisses, clicks, squeaks, snuffles and grunts. At intervals I got off the boat to lie in the warm sea water, but then I feared puk-puks (crocodiles) slithering out of the mangroves to bite my legs and drag me under. At last a misty dawn broke and I heard the slapping of oars as the workboat approached. In the daylight we were able to gather logs and branches to push under the boat and lever her over her self-made sandbank into deeper water, and return to the ship.

Then, in 1961 in one of the Japanese ports, a Captain had an accident resulting in a shuffle of personnel on the coast. As a result I was promoted to Chief Mate of the little steamer "Fengtien."
Twenty three years old and Mate, I was well pleased with myself. The Captain, two senior engineers, and I were British, while the rest of the crew were from various parts of China, but the seamen were Tientsin, by reputation the very best.

"Fengtien," built West Hartlepool 1945

7: Wong Numbers.

On our first trip to Indonesia, the Philippines, Japan, Shanghai, and back to Hong Kong, the bosun Wong impressed me with his attitude and ability. A fine man but with a troubled mind. His father had been bosun, and when he retired he made his men promise to serve under the son, for a trial period. Now Wong explained that he needed to find some "business" to supplement the wages, or they would drift off to more enterprising bosuns. "Business" meant trading internationally in goods which were prohibited or highly taxed. "Business" was illegal or immoral, depending on your point of view, but to the Chinaman he was simply carrying his own cargo, trading, supplying a need, just like the shipowner.

I straight away made it clear that I wanted no part of this nefarious activity, though I did want to keep our excellent seamen. Wong evidently took encouragement from this, and in Hong Kong he approached me with a cautious smile.

"I find good business. Sailormen stay one more trip," he said.

I should have shut him up right there, but impulsively asked,

"What kind of business?"

His reply,

"Passengers to Djakarta," horrified me. A few transistor radios or watches maybe, but human beings as contraband, was something else.

"How many?" I croaked.

"Seven," he replied, and seeing my shocked reaction added, "Suppose one man, seven man, all same, but more profit."

The ten day passage to Djakarta always entailed water rationing. How could we feed and wash seven extra bodies? And what if one got sick and died? Overside at night presumably with a shackle round his ankle. Or if the sickness was infectious and spread through the ship, what then? Getting them on board in Hong Kong shouldn't be a problem. They could be filtered among the hundreds of coolies, hawkers, prostitutes, crew's families, and odds and sods which day and night swarmed over the ship. But how would seven Chinese evade discovery in Djakarta, where Customs and Immigration officials searched the ship before anyone else could come or go?

As the days unfolded I pondered these questions and many more, longing to confide in someone but knowing I could not. "Close mouth, catch no fly," as they say.

On the morning of departure Wong entered my cabin closing the curtain behind him.

"All on board," he announced, "no problem, hide away under steering flat," and he thrust a bundle of notes into my hand. I tried to give them back but Wong insisted.

"Must be you take share, half now, half Djakarta. Sailormen savvy you know 'bout this business."

Sick with worry I went about my duties, checking Bills of Lading, signing Mates Receipts, worksheets, stores delivery notes, invoices and so on. At last I reported to the Captain that all was ready for sea, but without explanation he declared that sailing would be delayed one hour to 1300 hours. I shrugged and left. By 1200 all but crew had gone, in their junks, sampans, and wallah-wallahs. The ship lay alone at her buoy, deep laden, sleek in the water, and aft, below the waterline under piles of old ropes and canvas cowered our pigeon passengers, in the dark lazarette. We waited. Not for long, with wailing sirens police boats came circling the ship and approaching the gangway with about ninety police cadets, led by two British Inspectors. I met them there.

"Chief Officer, we've had a tipoff you may have stowaways on board. We'd like to search."

"Certainly," said I, suitably shocked, "In ships it's generally fore to aft," and I led them to the bow, in the opposite direction to where our pigeons were concealed. The cadets, like blue ants, climbed the masts, crawled under deck cargo, and peered into spaces too small for the smallest Chinese dwarf. Not a hint did the Inspectors give me as to numbers they were seeking, or how detailed was their information, and the roll of notes, uncounted, was burning a hole in my pocket. When we came at last to the steering flat all eyes went to the padlock of the lazarette below.

"Open that bosun," I said, dry mouthed and sweating. The hatch was opened and a couple of cadets went down. One of the Inspectors lit a cigarette, offered me one, which I declined, and smiled, about to speak. Then a hand emerged from the hatch holding a fresh piece of orange peel, and like hounds scenting prey more cadets dived in, jabbering excitedly. Soon our passengers came out, skinny frightened wretches in dirty shorts and shirts, not seven but fourteen of them! Interrogation by the Inspectors in Chinese determined that these were illegal immigrants from China, in transit to Indonesia.

"Poor devils, we don't want them, better in a way they had gone with you. Now we have the bother of sending them back," sighed the Inspector. But who was responsible for them being here? A bucket with fourteen pairs of chopsticks found in the sailors' galley narrowed it down to the deck department. Then a small seaman shuffled forward.

"All my business," he muttered, and was hand-cuffed, thrown into a police launch and taken away. No one seemed to question how one man could have organised and carried out this operation without others being involved. The ship was released and sailed at 1300hrs. On the pretext of checking cargo lashings I took the bosun into the hold, alone.

"Firstly take this filthy money!" I said. He took it, saying money would be needed to free his man, and pay the super.......

"Don't tell me," I interrupted sharply, fearing I would hear some Superintendent of Police, or perhaps our Marine Superintendent was corrupt. This whole damned business was a bog into which I had floundered and was sinking deeper. Oh to put the clock back. Then the bosun asked curiously if I had noticed a very white face during the police search. I had indeed, the Number One Fireman had looked ghastly.

"He jus' tol' me, every trip two man, in number five cofferdam, very good business."

So even as we spoke, way down in the ship's double bottom, in a cofferdam three feet deep, two feet wide, running across the ship from side to side between fuel and ballast tanks, two Chinamen crouched, whispering of a better future in another land.

On return to Hong Kong our Tientsin men were transferred to another ship, and replaced by a crew from Swatow, in south China.

I never again dabbled in "business." I henceforth took a higher moral stand, and left the business to those with more greed, and stronger nerves.

About this time my mother sent me a photograph she had taken outside the village church, of my former girlfriend's wedding. I suppose I should have anticipated it, but it hit me hard.

Any hopes I might have had of rekindling that relationship were now dashed completely. I suddenly realised what I was missing. When you pay cash for sex you buy, or hire, the ultimate intimacy, but there is no kissing, no meeting of minds, and little or no affection. You can't buy love. My life suddenly felt hollow, empty.

But there's no use wondering what might have been. "The moving finger writes, and having writ moves on…."

Then one day, berthed at Aji Kawa, Osaka, someone rushed into my cabin shouting that a seaman was in the water. My crew were painting overside on stages, and the man hooked around the stem, bowsed in so that he could paint the draught marks, had somehow fallen into the filthy dock water. Our Australian Second Mate, a strong swimmer, dove down several times but could not find the man. After an hour a diver came and brought the body up and laid it on the quay. I was taken away to the police station to answer a lot of questions in my poor Japanese and their poor English. They were surprised that I didn't know if he could swim. I explained that all seamen have to do those jobs; no man is treated or paid differently whether he can swim or not. Bureaucracy finally satisfied I was returned to the ship, where I found the crew in uproar. Their shipmate was still lying on the quay, with mouth open, one eye closed, and the other staring at the sky, while cargo work continued around him. I gave orders to the Japanese to cover the body and show respect while I reported to the Captain on my interview with the police. When I emerged I found the crew still very upset. Dirty rush mats had been thrown over the corpse, and four posts set in concrete placed around him to keep vehicles away. This time I protested vehemently that the body should be removed to a morgue pending a proper funeral, and I waited on the dock for the hearse. To my disgust, and Chinese fury, a yellow three wheeled pick-up arrived as if to collect so much rubbish! At long last a proper black ambulance came and men in uniforms gently loaded and took away the body.

In view of the initial shoddy treatment of the deceased foreign seaman we persuaded the Agent to lay on a proper service in a temple, followed by a dignified cremation. I represented the ship and Company, escorting the whole deck department in a bus to these ceremonies, and translating where possible. An awkward moment arrived when we were supposed to take a flower from a bucket and drop it in the coffin as we filed past and said our last farewells to our shipmate. The crew shied away, but I persuaded them he was, "all same sleeping." How wrong I was! He was wrapped in a white shroud which covered his open mouth, but that one eye still stared upwards, and his dirty paint spattered straw hat had been placed on his ankles, seeming to mark him even in death, as just a seaman, of no account.

I had a good drink that night.

A couple days later a box wrapped in pink paper and tied with ribbon was delivered to the ship containing, "sailor's bones." We gave it to the bosun for delivery to the family of the deceased in Hong Kong. But next day the bosun protested,
 "No man can do sleeping. Have got friend on messroom table." It was transferred to the Captain's cabin.

After fourteen months in that ship as Mate, without a break, I was sent home for leave. I had been away for three and a half years and had a lot of money. In London I bought a red Austin Healey sports car with black leather upholstery. With a red and black shirt to match I was the playboy of the village. I studied for and passed my Master's Foreign Going Certificate, and played another season of rugby for South Molton. I also met and married my first wife.

China Nav. Co. wives generally lived in Hong Kong, Auckland, or Sydney, and we decided on Sydney where I installed my wife in a flat, introduced her to colleagues' wives, and returned to sea.

Wives and children could occasionally accompany husbands to sea, and when I was mate of the passenger/cargo ship "Changsha," my wife and first child came with me around the Australian coast.
Walking in to Melbourne one day with the child in her pushchair, we crossed a road towards the Sir Charles Hotham Hotel, named after a former State Governor. It had seen better days. Just as we reached the pavement the batwing doors of the hotel burst open and a man was thrown out, narrowly missing us, and wrapping himself around a lamp post to avoid falling among the traffic. My wife shuddered with disgust and hurried on, but I called her back, saying I thought I knew the man. I approached him, searching my memory, and asked,
 "Were you ever in the "Cornish City?"
 "I was!" He replied thickly while trying to focus.
 "And did you leave us in Newcastle? (N.S.W.)
 "I did!" said he, frowning.
 "Gosh! We thought you were dead." I exclaimed.

"Well I'm not f'…ing dead yet!" He growled, spitting noisily. My wife was giving me one of her "poo," looks, as if she had trodden in dog's mess, so I left my old shipmate with his lamp post, and resumed our walk into town, while I explained.

We had had a contract to carry three cargoes of coal from Newcastle, just north of Sydney, to Japan. The crew soon drew their wages up to the hilt to finance boozing in Australia, and boozing and whoring in Japan. Then one evening this crewman was found changing English five-pound notes in the Cosmopolitan Hotel. Asked where he got them he said, "From the Captain," which was soon disproved. Then one of the more prudent seamen found that his stash of English money had been stolen. That evening the thief received a terrible beating. When I was sent to see why he hadn't turned to in the morning, I found him curled up in his bunk, with his head grotesquely swollen, eyes closed, and his face like rotten fruit, blue, black, yellow, green, and red. The following night he disappeared without trace, and had still not been found on our third and final call. He had either jumped ship, or been quietly dropped over side, with a shackle to sink him.

8: Uncle Frank.

For several years I had been trying to find my missing uncle, checking electoral rolls in various States, but with no luck. Then one of our passengers, having read the two precious letters I had from Frank to his sister, my mother, written from Murwillumbah, Queensland, in 1926, offered to help. Eventually he discovered that Frank had been laid off from the farm in the depression and had ended up in a mental hospital, to which I was directed for more information. This is the letter I received from the hospital superintendent:-

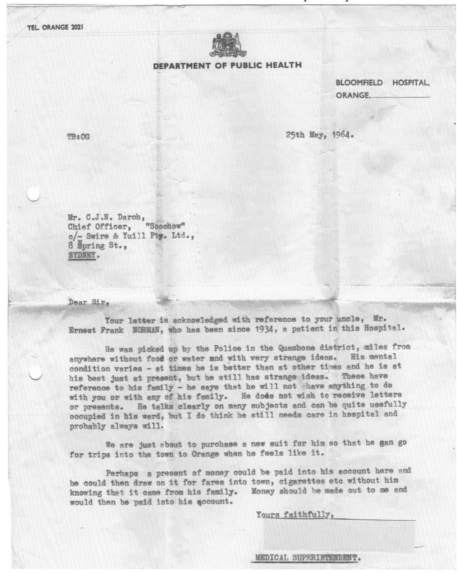

TEL. ORANGE 2021

DEPARTMENT OF PUBLIC HEALTH

BLOOMFIELD HOSPITAL,
ORANGE,

TB:OG

25th May, 1964.

Mr. C.J.N. Darch,
Chief Officer,   "Soochow"
c/- Swire & Yuill Pty. Ltd.,
8 Spring St.,
SYDNEY.

Dear Sir,

　　　　Your letter is acknowledged with reference to your uncle, Mr. Ernest Frank NORMAN, who has been since 1934, a patient in this Hospital.

　　　　He was picked up by the Police in the Quambone district, miles from anywhere without food or water and with very strange ideas. His mental condition varies - at times he is better than at other times and he is at his best just at present, but he still has strange ideas.   These have reference to his family - he says that he will not have anything to do with you or with any of his family. He does not wish to receive letters or presents.   He talks clearly on many subjects and can be quite usefully occupied in his ward, but I do think he still needs care in hospital and probably always will.

　　　　We are just about to purchase a new suit for him so that he can go for trips into the town to Orange when he feels like it.

　　　　Perhaps a present of money could be paid into his account here and he could then draw on it for fares into town, cigarettes etc without him knowing that it came from his family. Money should be made out to me and would then be paid into his account.

　　　　　　　　　Yours faithfully,

　　　　　　　MEDICAL SUPERINTENDENT.

Some years later I was informed that he had died. What a tragic life for a young man who had the spirit of adventure and the courage to travel across the world to find his fortune.

Uncle Frank on the farm at Murwillumbah, Queensland in 1926.

9: Passengers.

While I was serving in "Changsha" the Company offered a prize of HK$100 for economy suggestions, and I felt, with my thrifty tramp-ship background I could surely come up with something good. I soon targeted the "basket fenders" their ships had traditionally used. They were hand-made from rattan, intricately woven in Hong Kong. They worked well for small ships but as the Company's ships got bigger, including some heavy ones they chartered in, these fenders could not stand up to the extra stress put upon them. Overnight they could be crushed and rendered useless

So I typed up a proposal to seek out more robust fenders, probably of heavy rubber, to replace these picturesque "baskets." Proud of my suggestion I took it to my Captain for his endorsement. A man whose mantra was, "You can't be too careful," he offered me a seat and a gin and tonic while he read my letter. At last he said,
"Yes, yes, very good. But in my view you should not send this in. You might win yourself a hundred dollars, but you could do yourself incalculable harm, yes incalculable harm!"
I could not understand how my clever idea could do me harm, rather than be rewarded by praise.
Old John cautiously explained.
"You could stop the turkey over the wall."
"What turkey? What wall?" I asked naively.
"Well somebody, highly placed in Hong Kong, suddenly finds at Christmas, a turkey comes over his wall. He don't know where it came from. He can't send it back. But it is very welcome." Then suddenly these turkeys stop coming, and he wonders why. Eventually he realises he hasn't been ordering any more basket fenders. Perhaps there is a connection. And who was responsible for that? Young Darch, the clever dick, a name to be remembered.
I screwed up my smart suggestion and tossed it in the bin.

The "Changsha" carried eighty five passengers and I was never really comfortable with this part of our cargo. They sometimes got me into trouble. On one occasion travelling down through the Moluccas bound for the Torres Strait we had no sun or star sights for three days, it being overcast and hazy, and we were threading our way through shoals with no recognisable radar targets. A passenger at my table asked how this affected our navigation, and all the others leaned forward to listen. It was a sensible question and I gave a truthful answer, explaining that under those circumstances we navigated with caution until we could positively identify our position.

Within an hour I was summoned to the Captain's cabin.

" There's a rumour going round the ship that the Chief Officer says we are lost! Whatever have you been saying?"

On another occasion in Hong Kong, the Captain showed me a piece in the South China Morning Post. An American nightclub entertainer had been found dead from heroin overdose. Her distraught flat mate was to be one of our passengers to Australia. Our Chinese doctor was to keep a close watch on her including controlling her intake of narcotic substances. For the first week at sea the girl stayed in her cabin, no trouble at all. But then one evening our pretty nurse came to tell me the doctor was worried about "that girl." She was in a very agitated state parading about the aft deck in her night club clothes, fishnet stockings, turkey feathers, the lot, and he feared she might jump over the side. I got the nurse to bring her to my cabin and when she arrived I could see she was very much alive. She draped herself over my leather arm chair with much adjusting of long legs and flirtatious glances. We had a couple of gin and tonics and she smoked some cigarettes through an elegant holder, while the nurse discretely came and went, pretending other duties. Eventually we persuaded the young lady it was bedtime. The three of us descended to her cabin in steerage. She had a basic tubular steel bed, alone in a cabin normally occupied by four. While the nurse helped her undress I turned my back on them and busied myself screwing up the portholes really tight to prevent her taking that route into the sea. Then the nurse and I sat on stools at head and foot, stroking her hair and whispering to lull her to sleep. But every time we rose silently to leave the girl's eyes snapped open and targeted me. At last I signalled for the nurse to leave, took off my shoes and shorts, got into bed and attended to her evident urgent need. By the time I had dressed again she was snoring gently, and I let myself out of the cabin, confident that the therapy had worked.

Technically I had committed an act of infidelity, but it was obviously in the line of duty, and I never went near her again for the remainder of the voyage. The doctor gave me an enigmatic Chinese smile and a nod when I said she had needed a doctor of philosophy rather than a doctor of medicine.

10:Japanese.

I was still sailing to and from Japan, and my young friend Noriko continued to encourage me with the language. She persuaded me that if I wanted to make real progress I would have to learn to read and write in katakana, hiragana, and kanji, the scripts based upon Chinese characters. So with her help I embarked upon that lifelong task.

The Swire Group in the East encouraged their ex patriot office employees to learn local languages, and paid bonuses to those who could pass exams in Mandarin, Cantonese, and Japanese. When this concession was extended to the "floating" staff, I was the first to go to Tokyo and pass the Japanese examination. After the exam the examiner, Sorley, took me to the International Press Club for lunch, and explaining my fascination with Japan I mentioned my aunt and uncle Randall Hargreaves living there before the war. To my delight Sorley remembered Hargreaves doing occasional work for the BBC.

The Company reduced the length of tours, and after two and a half years my wife and I with our little girl, born in Australia, went home for leave. I enjoyed a third season of rugby with South Molton, but in various ways this leave was not a complete success. Adjusting to married life was not easy. My wife did not relish the thought of another long spell in Australia, but I was very happy in the China Navigation Company, and was due for promotion to command, so it made sense to go back. We visited an old school friend who had bought a smallholding in Wales and had a few Jersey milking cows. He explained that he needed to expand, but could not afford more cows, or the cost of employing labour. One solution would be to take a partner who would inject capital and work harder than an employee. The germ of an idea was born.

We returned to Sydney, found another flat, and I went back to sea. In March 1967 another beautiful daughter was born to us in Sydney, and in April, aged twenty nine I was promoted to command.

11:First Command.

My first ship was the "Chekiang," the first C.N.Co. ship I had ever seen, and I had sailed in her as Third and Second Mate, with happy memories. My first trip as Captain was to Bangkok, Singapore, various New Guinea ports, Fiji, Samoa, Tahiti, Japan, and back to Hong Kong. I had an excellent Chief Mate and Chief Engineer and all went well.

Master, April 1967

M.V."Chekiang," GT 5904 Built 1957 at Hong Kong. 4 cyl Doxford diesel
Speed 14.5 knots, single screw. Crew 8 British, 40 Chinese. 1983 Scrapped at Bombay.

I was two and a half years Master with C.N.Co., the time divided between "Chekiang," "Ninghai," and "Kweichow."

 Typhoons were a frequent problem and I had one serious incident while in the "Ninghai." We had left Hong Kong in a hurry and not quite ready for sea, as a typhoon approached. We managed to get all the derricks down and stowed and hatch covers in place and battened down, but as night fell and the seas built up I was conscious of the fact that mooring ropes were still coiled on the fo'c'sle head instead of being stowed below. During the night the wind steadily increased and I was obliged to heave to with the ship head to wind and sea, with speed adjusted to ride up over the mounting swells, and fall comfortably down the other side, without burying ourselves too deeply and risking damage. However at daylight we could see that one mooring rope had washed partly over the starboard side with the threat of it all going into the water, and possibly getting entangled around our propeller, leaving us disabled, a log upon the sea. I had to send the Mate and deck crew forward to retrieve the mooring rope and pass it and all the others down off the exsposed fo'c'sle head into the shelter below. I explained that I would do my best with engine and helm to keep from submerging their work area, but if I saw a particularly huge sea approaching I would warn them by loud blasts on the foghorn, and they were to leave the ropes and take shelter immediately.

I counted the men as they straggled up the deck by means of lifelines previously rigged. The Mate, Bosun, and seven seamen, in black oilskins and sea boots. I concentrated on the seas ahead, coming at us like streets of houses. With one of our best helmsman at the wheel and myself at the engine telegraph I eased her up and over and down into the troughs time and again, until I saw one huge "greybeard" advancing, standing taller than all the rest, meaning we would rise higher and plunge deeper than before. I pulled hard on the whistle line producing a deep roar from the horn on the funnel, but to my absolute horror no head was raised on the bow, they just kept passing the ropes as the ship reared up and then dove under the sea. The howling wind had clearly hidden my signal. After what seemed an eternity the bow and whole foredeck appeared streaming water, and I could see bodies scattered down the deck clinging to ropes, rails, bollards, and winches. I counted one here, three there, two over there, at last nine altogether. We could so easily have lost men overside, with no hope of rescuing them in that tumultuous sea. The Mate and Bosun put safe the last rope and then they all came aft to the safety of the accommodation. I had had a serious fright and learned a lesson, not to depend on a sound signal alone to warn men in a typhoon.

It was in that ship that we were obliged to spend a couple of weeks in Taiwan, the port of Keelung, including the Chinese New Year holiday. Our company's manager for Taiwan was Dawson Kwok, a tall imposing figure like a guardsman with a clipped moustache. He invited me, with the Chief Engineer and Mate, to a New Year's Day party at his grand house in Taipei. It was a gathering of important people who knew how close Dawson was to Madam Chiang, wife of the Generalissimo Chiang Kai-shek, President. Dawson and Madam Chiang served on committees of various charities, and he explained how that morning his first duty had been to deliver his New Year's Greeting to Madam Chiang. He then dramatically produced a peanut in shell which the lady had given to him. The Chinese gasped in admiration, aware of the significance of the peanut gift, which had to be explained to us foreign barbarians. It had something to do with time passing but true friendship never diminishing. When the peanut had served its purpose Kwok gave it to Eddie the Chief Engineer. On the way back to the ship I asked whether Eddie would have it mounted in a glass case, with a suitable inscription relating to Madam Chiang.

"Way no!" said Eddie, "I ate the booger!"

During this time I was studying farming books, and had some practical experience as we carried one thousand sheep on deck from Fremantle to Singapore, and another time took eighty in-calf Friesian heifers from Auckland to Manila, with a stockman to care for them. One calf was born in the San Bernardino Passage before reaching Manila meaning that our cargo manifest was in error by one animal. The problem was resolved in the usual manner, a gratuity.

My wife became pregnant with our third child and went home a little before me. Then in 1969, after eleven happy years with the China Navigation Company I resigned. The officers of my last ship, "Kweichow," gave me a pewter mug inscribed with best wishes for retirement, and I returned to England to be a farmer.

Farming and seafaring have a few things in common. They are both seriously affected by weather, and daily tasks are the same, with no exceptions for Sundays or Bank Holidays. Accidents and emergencies occur, and farmers and seamen tend to solve their own problems without resort to outside help.

12:A Spell Ashore

My old school friend had by this time moved into a sort of sub-tenancy in Hertfordshire and I joined him there, with wife, two daughters, and baby son. We milked seventy Jersey cows and had a few acres of barley and kale. Calves were being born all the time and we gave two of them Japanese names, Reiko and Rumi. Rumi was a particularly pretty little heifer and in her first lactation showed signs of being an exceptional cow. But one day she was hurrying up some granite steps, (I don't know why), and trod on her tits. The resulting damage left one quarter of her udder permanently dry. This was a sad loss.

We never got around to formalising our "partnership," and my wife and I increasingly worried about our finances. The outcome was that we left my friend and his family in Hertfordshire and moved into his small holding in Carmarthenshire. After transporting young stock to join the main herd I made all the hay I could to sell in the winter, and prepared the little farm for sale the following year, in accordance with a mutually agreed plan.

In the meantime I needed wages and my old friend John Williams came to my aid.
John was a lecturer at Warsash Navigation College, attached to Southampton University. He informed me that they required a second-in-command for the school's 78 ton training sloop "Halcyon." So I applied and got the job, driving down from Wales early every Monday and back Friday evening. With a crew of four we took fifteen pre-sea cadets sailing in the English Channel, with nights in Weymouth, Gosport, Cherbourg, and elsewhere. When the boys were not being sea-sick we taught them navigation, chartwork, the Rules of the Road, and seamanship.
That job lasted one school term of three months and then I was invited into the College to teach various classes, but with special responsibility for two Gambian River pilots, who were being groomed to take over from the British Harbourmaster in Banjul. They were only a couple years younger than me and we got along famously. They studied hard and listened carefully to all I taught them. One day I explained that in taking over a watch you never accept the position given you without checking it personally, as "no one is infallible." Up went a black hand,
"Sah, the Pope is infallible!"
"Well," I said, "I've never sailed with the Pope, but with the possible exception of him, you should treat everyone else as being capable of mistakes."

My second term at the College ended and I was released to return to the little farm. Still needing an income I applied for work at the Llyn Brianne dam under construction nine miles up the valley. Completely ignorant of anything on a huge project of this nature I was put with a motley gang picking up stones. It was a rock-fill dam with a clay core stretching across the valley and when I started the clay strip was hundreds of yards from side to side, and about one hundred yards front to back. A constant stream of tip lorries delivered the clay which contained some stone ranging in size from rugby balls and television sets to motor cars. Where possible we stone pickers carried the stones away from the clay, and otherwise called upon a D-6 bull dozer to help. Not wishing my mates to know a sea captain could come down to stone picking for a living. (They might have assumed I had wrecked a ship or been sacked for alcoholism or something), I just said, "I used to go to sea," and happily accepted the nickname "Sailor." I worked night shifts which left me free in the day to prepare the farm for sale. Most of the stone pickers were students, tramps, feckless characters who came and went without warning. With a wife and children to support I was the exception, never missing a shift. Because of this, when the waterman quit I was promoted to his work. This consisted of moving very long lengths of hose up and down the dam to wet the clay making it easier for big vibrating rollers to tamp it down. As a seaman I had no problem keeping the hoses running free and clear of kinks.

I was then offered a better paid job with the sub -contractors whose task was to quarry eighty thousand tons of rock per week to build the dam. I was a sort of "powder monkey" driving a tractor and trailer around the site, on day shift, replenishing the big Gardner-Denver drills with diesel, gear oil, and hammer oil, to keep them working non -stop. Then at the end of the shift I helped the shot firer charge the holes with gelignite, cordtex fuse and a mixture of ammonium nitrate and diesel, which was exploded by a battery and switch. When the site was clear a hooter sounded and with a loud double bang a whole shipload of rock erupted from the quarry face and fell in a heap, to be scraped up and transported to the dam in Euclid trucks of 27 cubic yard capacity.

If rock production exceeded 80,000 tons per week we all got a bonus. The boss decided the night shift were letting us down so he put the shot firer on nights to get more work out of them, and considered me capable of firing the shots without assistance! The" sailor" was coming up in the world.

The holes to be fired were 70 feet deep, four and five inches in diameter, and generally in two rows. All holes were connected by fuse cord with detonators selected to blow out the front row a split second before the back row, hence the double bang. Rock strata is not uniform so sometimes there were "toe-holes" to be drilled in stubborn lumps at the base of the cliff. These had to be charged with rods screwed together like drain rods to ram in the explosives. I was assured that everything was quite safe.

13:Return to Sea.

Spring came round, people viewed the farm, and eventually it was bought by a man and wife who bred horses and dogs, and he sold puppies at Harrods in London. I bade farewell to my mates at the dam, and prepared to return to sea. I went to London and joined the World-Wide Shipping Company of H.K. as Master on a twelve month contract. At the suggestion of the new farm owners my wife stayed on to help with the dogs, and I bought a forty two foot mobile home for the family to live in.

I flew to Tokyo and took over command of a bulk carrier, the "World Yuri." "Yuri" being Japanese for the "Lily" flower. The Mate, Chief Engineer, and Second Engineer were British, and the crew Chinese.

At one point we arrived in Vancouver and were told that a long planned stevedores' strike had commenced and we could expect to be there at anchor for many weeks. This presented me with a dilemma. As I was new to the Company I anticipated that a request to have my wife join me might be denied. So I got her to fly over at my expense and without notifying the Owners. It was something of a disaster. She was like a stranger, especially at night. I could not understand the change in her and she would not explain. When I confided in the Irish Mate, he merely laughed, saying, "Sure it's all part of the fun!"
This difficult situation lasted about two weeks until suddenly the Company ordered me to transfer to another ship. So I bundled my wife off home, handed over to the new Captain and flew to Japan to join the "Chiba," with a Korean crew.

A few months in the "Chiba" completed my one year contract and I took home leave. The problem with the wife was then revealed. A certain rep. used to circulate among the villages farms and pubs selling farm implements and second hand cars. He got to know my wife and among other things persuaded her to trade-in my old car for a better one of his. So in effect he screwed us both.
Clearly I had to relocate our family, so we moved back to Devon and bought a house near both sets of parents. My wife appeared happy with this situation and the children settled in to new schools.
But I believe our marriage had been damaged beyond repair, holed below the water, a constructive total loss.
Henceforth I suffered the usual fate of the cuckold, to be looked upon with contempt. Perhaps I would have retained my wife's respect if I had gone to fight over her, but I didn't. Feeling more despair than anger I hung my head in shame.

"Sometimes I wonder whether tolerance is mine or a rubber spine." Ambrose Bierce.

When my leave was up I was sent to Tilbury in the Thames to join "Eagle Glory," a bulker engaged in tramping, and my tour length was now reduced to ten months. The Chief Engineer and I were the only Europeans. The ship was registered in Panama and all the Chinese officers had Panamanian Certificates provided and paid for by the Company, and the rest of the crew were Koreans. The Chief Engineer had a Japanese wife who used to come and live on board whenever the ship was in Japan, and the three of us became firm friends.

With Atsuko, the Chief Engineer's wife.

One voyage was to Tubarao in Brazil to load iron ore. Six customs officers boarded to clear the ship, and after checking paperwork and noting the contents of my bonded store, they accepted a complimentary drink, and asked if they could buy whisky. As they were the authority I had no objection, so they opened their brief cases which each took six flat bottles of Ballantines scotch. The snag was that they paid me with a pile of Brazilian cruzeiroes with doubtful value outside of Brazil. The outcome was that I bought one large Alexandrite gemstone, which I subsequently had set in a gold ring in Singapore for my wife.

14: The Cellist

My ten month's tour of duty ended in Mizushima in Japan, and I was to fly to Hong Kong for de-briefing before going on to England.

Hong Kong was hidden in fog so the 'plane was diverted to Taipei where all passengers disembarked to the terminal. Eventually the flight was called again and among the throng of short orientals with black hair, a tall elderly European stood out. He had silvery hair swept back above a long forehead, aristocratic nose, and eyes and lips that twitched nervously. He appeared distressed and I felt compelled to help. He was greatly relieved and asked me to hold his cello case while he checked in his hand baggage. He explained that they always wanted to stow his cello in the hold of aeroplanes which he could not permit. While he checked in I studied the old grey battered cello case with hotel labels from various parts of the world. It had travelled far.

When we boarded the 'plane I was amused to see the old Frenchman apologising to left and right as he manoeuvred the case through the seats, and then sat with it on his lap.
Unfortunately Hong Kong was still fog-bound so we were directed on to Bangkok where we were taken to hotels for the night. The Frenchman and I checked in together and arranged to meet in the bar before dinner. When I found him there he was in conversation with a smart French lady and we had drinks together. Neither had been to Bangkok previously so they accepted my suggestion of dinner at a hotel beside the river, which had been a regular haunt of the writer Somerset Maugham. We spent a convivial evening chatting in English and French, and at one point he remarked that he appeared to have shrunk and his suit was hanging slack. I quoted T.S.Eliot.
"I grow old, I grow old, I shall wear the bottoms of my trousers rolled." The cellist was amused and whipped out a note book to write it down, saying that he had met Eliot in Paris in the 20's.

Next morning I again took care of the cello at check in. During my three days in Hong Kong I saw posters advertising, "Famous French cellist, Paul Tortellier doing recitals." There were no pictures but I felt it must be him, and if he was famous the sophisticated French lady must have known who he was.

A couple of months later, at home, I saw that he was doing a late night interview with Jonathan Dimbleby, so I stayed up to watch. It was indeed my Frenchman and they discussed various aspects of Beethoven's music. One of Dimbleby's last questions was whether Beethoven would approve of Tortellier's cello. At this the maestro gave a withering look down his long nose and replied, "Of course! My cello was born **before** Beethoven!" I'm surprised he couldn't afford a seat for it.

15:Divorce.

"Femme de marin, femme de chagrin." As they say in France.

Unfortunately my wife had despaired of life with me, and had found an Irish corporal in the RAF to share her future. She and our three children left, with whatever they could pack into the corporal's car, including the ring which had cost thirty six bottles of Ballantines.

I then found employment closer to home, to keep in touch with the children. At the Hull Trinity House I was examined and granted a license as a Deep Sea Pilot for the North Sea and European coastal waters. The work entailed boarding ships inward bound to the Channel for ports bordering the North Sea and the Baltic. This was not a compulsory pilotage and the clients we served were generally from non European Companies, in exceptionally big ships, such as tankers of 275,000 tons with draughts of 72 feet, more or less maximum for transiting the Dover Strait and approaches to Rotterdam. We also did container ships and car carriers which had very tight schedules calling at several ports in a week or ten days. Between jobs we generally spent a week at home awaiting the next turn. I followed that rather gruelling routine for over twenty years with no particularly interesting incidents to record, except perhaps when I shipped as A.B. in an American ship.

 I had joined "Seatrain Washington," off Brixham and piloted her to Rotterdam and Bremerhaven, and learned from the Captain that after several months shuttling between European and Meditteranean ports, she was bound for Norfolk Virginia. Many of the American crew had gone home, for various reasons, and had been replaced by aliens from Spain, Israel, and Turkey, whom the Master now intended to fire, rather than take them to the U.S.A. Well, he sacked them all and applied to the American consul in Bremen for "genuine Americans." The consul produced only one, a WWll soldier on a sentimental visit to old battlefields, which had consumed all his money. This left the ship under-manned. The Captain suggested that I could,
"Ride with us. We'll put you down as A.B., and fly you home from Norfolk with a pocket full of dollars!" So I agreed.

The American Mercantile Marine is like no other merchant shipping. The ships are heavily subsidised by the government, protected from foreign competition on the U.S.A. coast, from Boston to Alaska including the Gulf of Mexico, by the Jones Act, and the crews are strongly unionised. Very little work is done. People sit around drinking coffee and playing cards. They have no alcohol at sea but make up for it in port. On my first two sea watches I took my turn at sitting in the ship's hospital nursing the bosun who was suffering from delirium tremens. He shook and muttered constantly, with occasional screams and whimpers. Once he called for Coca Cola but before I could get it he said,

"Don't worry, the guy in the top rack needs it more than me!" Needless to say there was no bed above him, or man in it.

The only work I did was to paint some boat deck railings. "It will help to pass the time." I was told. During some heavy weather I took my turn at the wheel and was amused to see how the Greek/American Second Mate found it difficult to give me orders having so recently taken orders from me. To put him at ease I asked him to teach me the Greek alphabet which he was pleased to do.

American A.B.s Discharge paper.

I look back upon that time as a rather arid period, though it did pay a decent wage, and gave me experience of all kinds of ships. As many of them were Japanese I kept up with the language, and in 1991 I passed an exam in Japanese & Japanese Studies, set by the University of Cambridge Local Examinations Syndicate. Also a second wife came into my life and left, being quite unsuitable.

Three of the many ships I took through the English Channel / North Sea between 1974 and
1999.Top to bottom, an ore carrier, an oil tanker, a car carrier (6,000 cars.)

16:M.S.Oldenburg.

The island of Lundy, off the North Devon coast, is served by the lovely ferry "Oldenburg" built in 1958 to run between the Friesian Islands and Heligoland. She carries supplies to Lundy, including sheep back and forth, and during the summer months up to 267 passengers. During 1995 and 1996 "Oldenburg's" captain was courting a new wife, and occasionally asked me to take over the ship so that he could visit her. This was normally for the two hour run out to the island from Bideford or Ilfracombe, and after a few hours there, back again. But on one occasion the ship was chartered by a BBC film crew to make an episode for a 999 programme. One of the RAF helicopter pilots at nearby Chivenor had previously been involved in a dramatic rescue of Chilean fishermen from a burning trawler somewhere between South Georgia Island and the Falkland Islands. He was now to take part in a re-enactment of the drama for the BBC. During the original incident a New Zealand scientist had been on board the fishing boat monitoring the amount of albatross caught in their longlines. He had lots of film footage including the dramatic helicopter rescue as the vessel burned and sank. But the film crew needed to supplement that footage and as the "Oldenburg" was of a suitable size and situated close to the pilot at Chivenor it made sense to hire her for a day.

We sailed from Bideford one morning in October in suitably wintry conditions, with an attractive young lady director, camera crew, and actors and extras chosen to look like Chileans. The man playing Captain was a cockney with an Italian mother. Pipes to emit smoke were fitted on the port side of our fore deck and I was asked to keep the wind on the port side, with no land in the background, and clear of other vessels. To achieve this I anchored off Clovelly with a full scope of anchor cable out on the port side. Thus, using our twin screws I could keep the ship steady with the wind coming over the bow. Then the fun began. There was much shouting and rushing about in the smoke, and the director called for more extras to add to the melee, but alas several of them were too sea sick to oblige. Those that were capable launched our inflatable liferafts and jumped into them carrying the ship's dog, in this case an extremely well trained dog from an agency. On instruction it would feign death, with eyes open, and tongue lolling out. Meanwhile the cockney Italian kept hollering,
"Abandanero el bawko!"

Then we heard the thrashing of helicopter blades and the chopper rescued the men from the liferafts and dropped them back on board, filming over. The lady director appeared well satisfied and we landed the nineteen of her party at Clovelly before returning to Bideford. It had been a thoroughly entertaining day, with money in the bank for the Lundy Company.

17:Trials Master, Appledore Shipyard.

As an occasional break from the pilotage I took the job as Trials Master for the local shipyard at Appledore, in North Devon. Between 1992 and 2003 I did the trials and delivery of 23 ships built at the yard.

 When a ship is built she remains the property of the builders until she has been put through sea trials under command of the builder's Captain. When she has performed to the satisfaction of the owner he then accepts the ship, and appoints his own Master and crew. Some of these trials take just twenty four hours, while others take a week or two, as in the case of ferries which have to dock at their operating ports, and dredgers which have to dredge in the rivers they were designed for. This gave me valuable experience in handling small ships with a variety of propellers, rudders, nozzles, and thrusters. The most prestigious ships I trialled for Appledore shipyard were "Roisin," and "Neame," fishery patrol ships for the Irish Navy, and "Scott," a survey ship for the Royal Navy. When they hauled down the red ensign and hoisted the white after trials of "Scott," which then became H.M.S., they presented me with the red one. It's a three yard flag which I hang from my balcony railings on occasions such as royal weddings.

"Scott," built at Appledore 1997. Shown here under red ensign before hand over to the Royal Navy and becoming H.M.S.Scott.

About this time I was extremely fortunate in meeting my present wife. She is a saint, possibly Saint Jude, the patron of lost causes and no-hopers. Her most saintly attribute is compassion, and unlike her predecessors she understands me.

She was my greatest support when my eldest daughter was killed in a car crash just before her nineteenth birthday. To lose any child is devastating, but she was the one I had known and loved the longest, and spent most time with. At her funeral I found that the strength of my un-belief sustained me. When tears threatened I was able to convince myself that Suzanne was totally gone for ever, and in that box was just cold meat and bones. Tears would only be through self-pity, pain at my great loss, and surely a man could control his self-pity?

18: Ship Delivery.

As a British North Sea pilot I used an agency which obtained the work, processed the bills, and sent a monthly share to the pilots who had contributed to the earnings. Eventually our agent retired and his business was acquired by a Dutch Company, Wijsmuller, who also undertook the delivery of ships all over the world. I had become weary of the North Sea and was glad of the opportunity to get back into the tropics, so I became one of Wijsmuller's delivery Masters.

Wijsmuller's business was mainly to take harbour craft, such as tugs, dredgers, small ferries, and workboats, which had been sold in one country, and to deliver them to new owners in another country, often on the other side of the world. As crew we never knew what the next job might be, and I found the variety and ever varying challenges enthralling. Also, after so many years as a pilot working with all types of Masters, sometimes timid or nervous, sometimes arrogant and over bearing, it was a relief to be once again in command. Through long experience Wijsmullers were expert at equipping these small craft for ocean voyages, and we knew that no expense was spared on food, communications or safety. For our part we had to economise with fuel, and make do with minimum crew, generally five or six in total. But these were first class seamen willing to put up with privations, bad weather, and lack of sleep. They were also an intriguing mix of nationalities, British, Dutch, Russian, Indonesian, Filipinos, Ghanains, Latvians , and so on.

Once the main details of routes and bunker ports had been decided, Masters were given wide discretion in terms of sheltering in ports of refuge, and deviations to avoid extremes of weather. But such was the esprit de corps the Company inspired there was a general desire to get the delivery done, safely and economically, and show a good profit.

Between 1999 and 2009 I delivered twenty eight ships, twenty of them under the Wijsmuller House flag, and they were happy years.

In December 2003 I went to Messina in Sicily to take a tug to new owners in Trieste, but they insisted on her fuel tanks being cleaned before arrival. Nobody in Messina would undertake this so we were ordered to Malta. The tank cleaning firm there closed for Christmas and New Year so I left the Mate in charge and went home. On New Year's eve my wife suggested joining the midnight celebrations in nearby Bideford where a firework display was planned. But first I did a tour of the bars and bazaars of Appledore and hurt my ankle so that I had to phone my wife for help. She was disgusted with me and sent me to bed early with no supper. The following day she suggested I sought medical advice but I didn't want plaster and crutches to prevent me completing the Trieste delivery. So when the tug was ready, with clean tanks, I took train and 'plane to Malta and did the three day passage to Trieste. In due course I arrived home and went to the hospital casualty department. A lady in white coat X-rayed the ankle and said the fibula was broken, but it was healing well. She then asked when the accident happened and when I said seventeen days previously she asked why I had taken so long to get treatment. I explained that I was working in a ship, which made it difficult. Then white coat asked whether the Captain had got medical help, and when I said no, she said he must have been a brute! I agreed, a callous pig.

Another delivery was the "Badzu Maru" named by the American owner after a character in a Japanese comic. This ship, of just 240 tons, had been a Royal Navy patrol boat engaged in Irish coastal waters during the "troubles," intercepting gun runners. But for several years she had been de-commissioned, laying in a berth at Southampton, under various owners and with very little maintenance. I was appointed Master with a crew of six, all British. We spent a week or so at Southampton preparing for sea, doing trials in the Solent, storing up, and getting to know each other over a few beers. There was some delay getting a special export license as she had been a warship and could be easily converted back to that role, but at last we set out, with first destination Punta Delgado in the Azores. All went well as far as there, although one of the two engines smoked a lot, and stuttered a bit while approaching our berth. After a pleasant day's stop-over we proceeded on the next leg to Bermuda, nine days away. Three days out the rudders jammed hard over so we had to stop and investigate. Fortunately the sea was glassy calm, with just a long oily swell to give us a moderate roll. The Chief Engineer and I spent several hours in cramped positions disengaging the starboard rudder from the port, to establish where the problem lay. There was some fear at that point that we would have to hand steer to Bermuda, six days ahead, or back three days to the Azores, with me opting for forward, and the young Mate voting for back. Fortunately the port rudder, hydraulically driven, was functioning well, so we continued, with starboard rudder disengaged. We spent three or four days in Bermuda overhauling the rudders and packing them with grease, while we also allowed some bad weather ahead to disperse. Taking a stroll over the island to Tobacco Bay I stopped to look at a church which had been abandoned before it was completed. An old black man chanced along, with a ring of white hair on his head which gave him a priestly aspect, so I asked him why the church had never been finished. He couldn't tell me, saying apologetically that history was not his strong subject. We speculated that the builders had probably run out of money, or faith. There are many examples of the faithful overcoming financial stringency to construct their places of worship, so I concluded that here they had more likely run out of faith. As he left me the old boy muttered that he guessed they had, "Sure just done runned out o' faith."

The weather from there to Baltimore, our final destination, was fickle but deteriorating, and conditions became severely uncomfortable in the convergence zone between the Gulf Stream and the inshore counter current.

The cook, a volatile character, appeared in the wheelhouse waving a frying pan around his head, threatening me with violence unless I chose a safer quieter course allowing him to keep his pots on the stove. Secured by rope to the wheel I could neither defend myself nor dodge the potential blows, while doing my best to nurse her through the confused sea which seemed intent on sinking us. Somehow we survived that and made it into port where our millionaire American owner was waiting. He required us to demonstrate the working of the ship over several days in the Chesapeake Bay while we spent the evenings exploring the local bars. All differences between me and the Mate and the cook were forgotten. I even had to support the cook's story as he chatted up a girl,

"I'm divorced wi' two kids!"

Whereas he actually had a wife and five children.

Another epic voyage was to collect two newly built work boats from Puerto Montt, in Southern Chile and deliver them to Warri in West Africa. Mine was 24 metres long while the other was just 17.

This time we had a mixture of British and Russian crews, with an elderly Dane as Chief Engineer of the smaller vessel. Ballast tanks were modified to take extra diesel for the long passages up to Panama Canal and across the Atlantic to the Cape Verde Islands, and finally Nigeria.

Absolutely stuffed to the brim with fuel we set out along the Chilean coast, headed north. Though the wind was moderate there was an amazing swell on the beam, coming from way out in the South Pacific. My ship rolled violently but I was very worried about the other as she fell out of sight in the troughs and then reared crazily into view on the crests. Two days out the Captain of the other reported that the old Dane had fallen in the Engine Room and by his own diagnosis had broken his femur. Incredibly he had crawled to his bunk and lay chain smoking until his relief had sought him at change of watch. We immediately diverted to Talcuahano, the port for Conception, which we reached a day later. The old Viking had actually broken his pelvic ring and had to be hospitalised for some weeks before flying back to Europe. When a new Chief Engineer arrived we continued up the coast to Panama.

At the Atlantic side of the Panama Canal in Cristobal we again took absolute maximum fuel and set out to the Cape Verde Islands off West Africa. Our plans anticipated a swift economical passage across the Caribbean but this was not to be, so the smaller ship had to put in to Georgetown in Barbados for extra fuel, while I stayed at sea to avoid port charges. I was later rewarded with a bottle of Mount Gay rum.

We made a reasonable crossing of the Atlantic, spent a couple days in Saint Vincent, Cape Verdes, resting up and bunkering, and then did the last leg to Warri, and Lagos, in Nigeria. Nigeria can be dangerous with pirates on the coast, armed robbers in port, corrupt officials, and generally lawless conditions, but we got through it unscathed.

One of my most enjoyable assignments was to fly out to the Falkland Islands and deliver an old tug to Cape Town. We first assembled at Punta Arenas in the Straits of Magellan, Brits, Dutch, and Russians. After twenty four hours of "crew bonding" in the hotel " Los Navegantes," we made the short flight across to Port Stanley. There I was reacquainted with my old cook, he of the whirling frying pan, who greeted me like a long lost brother. He had been working on the old tug "Indomitable," but would not be sailing with us to Cape Town. "Indomitable," had spent twenty years in the Falklands, chartered by the government but was now considered worn out, and was to be replaced. She had been sold to African interests. We spent some interesting days in the local pubs made famous by the Falklands war, the Globe, Victory, Rose, and Upland Goose. We also prepared the tug for sea. A big question was lubricating oil. Nobody seemed to know how much she would use on a long passage, having only dodged about the islands for twenty years. Lubricating oil was very expensive in Port Stanley so we resolved to take enough to get us to Montevideo five days north, by which time we could assess the daily consumption, and then take enough drums on board for the nineteen days steaming across to Cape Town.

We followed that plan and approached Montevideo at 2 0'clock in the morning. We berthed between enormous fish factory ships which came and went involving frequent adjustment of our mooring lines. It was a busy day but the Mate and I could not resist an evening run ashore, neither of us having been there before. My wife's uncle had been in the engine room of H.M.S. Exeter in the famous fight against the Graf Spee in the war resulting in her being scuttled just outside Montevideo, which gave me an added interest in the port. The wreck of the old German warship is still a hazard to navigation with buoys marking her position. Our tour of the bars was good, but when the Mate suggested a night club at midnight I protested that I needed sleep, having been up twenty two hours. I returned to the ship while the Mate carried on. Having been recently divorced after twenty odd years he was looking for action. In the morning he wasted some time finding a cash point to pay for the night's fun, so almost held up our departure.

The nineteen day run across due east to Cape Town was idyllic. Not a ship sighted, nor aircraft in the sky. Just beautiful lonely days and starry nights. The track took us a hundred miles north of Tristan Da Cunha but we had no indication it was there apart from the chart. That is what I most enjoyed about delivery work, the reminder of the vastness of the oceans. And being in such small ships one feels, hears, tastes, and smells the sea, passing through it rather than over it. I fully understand what Emily Dickinson meant:-

"Not born, like me among the mountains, can a sailor understand the divine intoxication, of the first league out from land?"

'INDOMITABLE'

Port of Registry Liverpool, Official Number 378072 Call Sign GYAJ

"Indomitable," Built 1979 GT 406 Length 104 ft. Bollard pull 70 tons.
In Falkland Islands 1987 to 2007

I was now in my seventieth year, and spent a quiet summer as one of the two summer Captains of the local ferry to Lundy Island. Two hours out, four or five hours there, two hours back, and every night at home, in domestic harmony with my sainted wife.

Seventieth birthday celebrations in the Lundy Island ferry "Oldenburg." 2007.

Perhaps I should have stayed there but when Wijsmuller offered me a job that winter I could not resist.

19:Pirated

The Ill-fated Delivery of "Svitzer Korsakov.

Two ice breaking tugs were under construction in St. Petersburg, and Wijsmuller, now renamed Redwise, had contracted to deliver them to the Far East. I was offered command of one of them named "Svitzer Korsakov," and accepted.

I applied for a Russian visa, and waited at home in North Devon, while information trickled through. Russia had opened up a new deepsea port in Sakhalin, a peninsula north of Japan, for the export of natural gas. Two icebreaking tugs built in Singapore were already working at the new terminal, while a second pair, for some political reason, had been commissioned from the Admiralty yard in St.Petersburg. This yard had not previously undertaken commercial work and was struggling to complete the ships on schedule, much to the frustration of the Danish tug owners Svitzer, part of a well known Danish conglomerate. They operate tugs in many ports of the world, and shuffling these tugs around provides the Dutch Company with a lot of work.

In some important respects this delivery was to be different. Svitzer requested, or insisted, that the Dutch should provide only a Master and Chief Engineer for each ship. The Mates and Second Engineers, and two Able Seamen for each tug were to be Svitzer men, all Russians from Sakhalin. Our contract was to deliver the tugs to Singapore where they were to be drydocked for any defects and deficiencies to be corrected before proceeding to Sakhalin. Our involvement was to end on arrival Singapore, and the Mates and Second Engineers would be promoted to Masters and Chief Engineers for the last leg of the delivery, and would in future operate the tugs at the gas terminal.

The joining date was put back several times, and we went on to three quarters pay.

At last on 6th December 2007 we flew to St.Petersburg and gathered at the Hotel Anushka. Joe Benneton from Newcastle was to have command of "Svitzer Busse" with a Liverpool Chief Engineer, and I was to have the "Svitzer Korsakov" with Ted Burke from the west of Ireland as Chief Engineeer. Benneton had served as Mate with me on an oil rig supply boat delivered from Cameroon to Dubai, and we were good friends. The fifth member in the hotel was our Dutch boss, a fine gentleman who had decided to personally superintend this contract rather than send a subordinate, in view of the unusual nature of the crewing, and other factors.

69

On 7th December we visited the tugs for the first time, driven by a Russian agent in a mini bus. Due to strict security in the Admiralty shipyard we had to enter and leave together with all five names on one pass.

My ship was more advanced than the other but both needed a lot done to be ready for sea. We were introduced to the two chief Mates, Igor for "Busse" and Nikolai Berezovskiy for me. Berezovskiy, tall, hunched, with thick black moustache, dull unsmiling eyes, and heavily accented English. Igor said little. These men, and the two engineers, had been standing by the construction of the tugs for three months, including the sea trials, so could be expected to have a thorough knowledge of them. Berezovskiy reported that the trials had been satisfactory, apart from one or two glitches, for example the port anchor of the "Korsakov" had been damaged and replaced. Svitzer were impatient to get the ships out of Russia and had arranged for most of the stores to be deposited at Fredericia in Denmark, where we were to spend four days storing up, doing bollard pull trials, and finishing off other essential work.

On 8th December we decided to leave the ships to the painters and cleaners swarming over them, and visit the Hermitage Museum. I particularly wanted to see the Gauguins having been to the little Gauguin museum in Tahiti in the 1960s. The time spent in the Hermitage was simply wonderful, a real boost to morale before facing the rigours of the sea.

On 10th December we checked out of the Anushka Hotel and went cheerfully aboard, but were disappointed to find the ships still not ready to live in. This day we met the two Second Engineers, to become Chief Engineers on arrival Singapore. Both named Alexander, and mine Lichkunov struck me as the more pleasant of the pair.
Before returning to the hotel our boss invited Igor and Nikolai to join us for dinner and drinks, a chance to break the ice and get to know each other. They did not come.

On 11th December the four seamen arrived from Sakhalin, and Berezovskiy introduced me to mine, Pyotr Kimochkin and Evgeny Komkov. Neither spoke English and when I enquired which was the cook they looked at their feet and muttered. Berezovskiy grunted, "They will share." Back at the hotel I learned from Joe Benneton that he also had no cook, though one of his A.B.s spoke reasonable English having worked on North Sea oil rigs.

December 12th was a very busy day on which Benneton and I officially took command of our ships, after lengthy grilling by officials on our knowledge of ISM and ISPS rules. These have to do with safety management and port security. Finally satisfied, the officials issued the necessary certificates for us to sail.

All hands then took stores sufficient for the four day passage to Fredericia, and after a hard day with nothing to eat or drink we returned to the hotel, too late for dinner. The boss eventually persuaded them to provide soup and salad.

December 13th we quit the hotel and moved aboard to complete preparation for sea. For days I had been urging Berezovskiy to mobilise the men to get the ship secured for sea. Maindeck porthole deadlights to be screwed down, accommodation windows to have steel plates bolted over them, tank ventilators to be covered with canvas bags, and all loose equipment in the ship to be lashed down. His response was always,

"Yes, yes, of course!" implying that all was in hand. Yet on this day I found very little done, and no sign of Nikolai Berezovskiy. Then I collided with him in long leather boots beneath a greatcoat, with gold buckle and buttons, and enormous flat board epaulettes with four wide gold bars. Ignoring the Captains' insignia, not due him until Singapore, I brought him up short with stern advice.

"Get out of that ridiculous pantomime costume, get yourself on deck with those other idle bastards, and get this vessel ready for sea! And if you Russian cretins don't understand I'll send you back to Outer Mongolia and hire some real seamen from Finland or Poland!"

I knew he would not catch all the words, but when words fail music speaks, and I hoped my tone would sting him into action. The boss hinted that Russians respond well to being shouted at. Well that is not my style, this is not the army nor the royal navy. When battening down a small ship for a winter passage the old adage applies, "Take care of your ship and your ship will take care of you." True seamen know that and do it without bullying.

That night we slept on board, expecting a morning departure.

December 14th I was up early making final checks. The plan was to move down the river Neva to a commercial wharf where port officials would board for departure formalities, and issue our Outward Clearance. Accordingly a pilot boarded Svitzer Busse at 1000. She was to leave the berth first with me following close behind. But suddenly the Busse surged back and her stern roller put a deep half round dent in my icebreaker bow. A bad start.

Then Busse was off like a frighted steed, into mid river, twisting and turning erratically, but gradually moving downstream. I was about to cast off when an anxious call came from Joe

71

Benneton reporting his controls unreliable. Not trusting them he set everything to neutral, and drifted slowly down river while I was instructed to go to him, lash up alongside, and bring him back to the shipyard berth. This I did very cautiously, aware of the great power of the engines, and very sensitive controls.

Shipyard experts piled aboard to check the computerised controls, engine settings, monitor readings, and finally their trials Master did a short trial in the river, and pronounced everything in good working order.

So at 1630 we set out again and berthed head to stern at a commercial wharf, for the Port Officials to do their stuff. To ease the way the agent laid on bottles of vodka to supplement the ship's beer. A jolly crowd of officials bunched up in our little tugboat messroom. Half a dozen men and one lady, who could have been Kruschev's twin, with uniforms buttoned up to their double chins and red faces shiny with sweat. Svitzer Busse had a similar valedictory party, and we cast off at 2200.

The passage down river between rows of ships, with occasional passing traffic required all my concentration, hands on port and starboard thruster controls, eyes moving between radar, echo sounder, RPM and pitch indicators, and a patch of floodlight ahead which showed thick plates of ice. Sometimes the pilot indicated with a raised finger to pass one side or the other of these obstacles which thudded against the hull. Few words passed between us in the darkened wheelhouse, but we worked well together, until the bulk of Berezovskiy intruded, breathing like a bear.

"Don' worry Captain!" his greeting as he lurched against me reaching past to change the radar range. The pilot and I ignored him as he fumbled around in the dark and bumped me again while adjusting a dimmer switch or something.

"Nikolai, I'm quite happy with the settings, if you want to help get us some coffee!"

"Don' worry Captain," he retorted thickly. The atmosphere was tense. The Russian pilot spoke no word to his compatriot. If he had suspected the Mate of being drunk he should have reported it to Port Control resulting in a visit from Harbour Police, involving delay and possible detention. I willed the Mate to be quiet.

Soon after midnight we reached Kronshtadt where the pilot disembarked, and at 0230 I judged Berezovskiy fit to take charge of the ship, so handed over to him and went to bed.

The next three days at sea were uneventful apart from Joe reporting intermittent problems with his autopilot. Neither of us was happy with the food situation but we put this down to poor provisions supplied for the short trip to Fredericia, to be remedied once our Dutch stores came aboard. As the nominated "Commodore" of this flotilla of two I had to make daily progress reports to Holland, and found the Russian computer difficult. Nikolai Berezovskiy helped but preferred to work through his personal laptop rather than the ship's equipment, so I arranged for the standard Satcom C in a suitcase to be supplied by the Dutch, at Fredericia.

We spent six days in Fredericia with both tugs undertaking bollard pull trials, trying to achieve the 70 tons pull required by the owners. When we had a chance we also took stores. There were many cases in a warehouse, containing food, paint, various types of oil, spare engine parts, and equipment for the owner's depot at Singapore. A Danish forklift driver carried these crates to the ships'side for our crews to crane them aboard and stow for sea. Much time was spent sorting the boxes in the warehouse, and as Christmas approached, everyone was anxious to get us out before the holiday. To save time I ordered that so long as we got an equal number of cases we would sort it out later.
"If we get all the beans and "Busse" gets all the peas, so be it!" Engine and electronic experts steadily leached away to Russia, Norway, Sweden, Holland, Lithuania, and even one to Iceland. On Christmas Eve in the morning we were cast off and Denmark went into holiday mode.

Our destination Kiel canal, to make a Christmas Day transit into the North Sea, but this was not to be. Approaching Holtenau at the Baltic end of the canal Joe Benneton reported starboard engine alarm systems malfunctioning. So we berthed at Nordhafen, just inside the canal, and there we stayed. No technical advice available on Christmas Day. Hamburger and chips for lunch. In the evening Chief Engineer Ted Burke and I walked to a Seamens' Mission, where a little old lady in tatty slippers let us in and served coffee, there being no alcohol. Ted connected up his laptop and sent greetings home, while I found A.N.Wilson's biography of C.S.Lewis, and read a couple of chapters.

On Boxing Day an expert telephoned and talked the" Busse's" Chief Engineer through some adjustments to his engine alarm systems, which appeared to cure the problem. On 27th December both ships topped up fresh water tanks, and proceeded down the Kiel canal, but Joe soon reported auto pilot trouble, and was obliged to hand steer most of the way. When I relayed this information to Holland they instructed us to enter Ijmuiden, to get this, and all of "Svitzer Busse's" various faults thoroughly checked. I was much relieved, suspecting that the "Busse" had been hastily completed and sent to sea in an unsatisfactory condition.

The Kiel canal exits into the river Elbe at Brunsbuttel and from there to Ijmuiden in Holland involves rounding the Texel where we got a real bashing from short seas and high winds. One of my temporary freezers was smashed up, some lubricating oil drums worked loose, fractured, and lost contents, and my heavy wooden bunk broke away from the bulkhead and sashayed about the cabin, making sleep impossible. Not requiring a pilot we entered Ijmuiden and berthed in the early hours of 29th December.

Captain Benneton and I had a conference. We both wanted to change the entire crew for reliable company's men, but knew that would not be possible. Instead we decided to insist on having cooks. Our seamen had no idea about food preparation or hygiene. They preferred to open tins of fish and meat to eat cold with cheese, onions and bread, leaving fresh vegetables to waste.

A large pan stood on the stove all day containing water, scraps of cabbage and lumps of meat and bones, from which we could ladle a portion at any time, except at night when it cooled. We called it "Gulag soup." Joe's English speaker understood when asked to cook eggs or potatoes in different ways, but I had to pass these requests through Berezovskiy, with the usual response,

"Yes, yes, Of course!"

Joe's Mate Igor was so unsure of his English that he passed mandatory reporting points in silence. So Joe and I decided to stand opposite watches so that one Company Master was awake at all times and could speak for both ships when challenged by coastguards, oil platform guardships, survey ships towing seismic cables, and other hampered vessels. Although Svitzer ships are dry we agreed this was a Dutch operation and we would share the beer with the Russians, hoping to build goodwill and team spirit.

That evening Ted and I walked across low sandhills to a small beach resort where we had beer and a fish meal. Then we gatecrashed a 35th wedding anniversary party, and were made very welcome by Dutch who reminisced about the war.

Sunday 30th December. Someone from the Company turned up to photograph our storm damage, and assess what expert technicians were needed to sort out the problems, mainly on "Svitzer Busse" to finally prepare us for sea. Received replacement oil drums and a new deep freezer to replace the smashed one, and topped up fresh water tanks.

Monday 31st, New Year's Eve. Ted and I took a stroll ashore but found nothing open so returned aboard. Approaching midnight we gathered together in the messroom, all six crew of the "Korsakov". The Russians produced some vodka and cheese and we toasted the old year, the new year, and the voyage ahead. At midnight, being the oldest on board, aged seventy, I rang out the old year with eight bells, followed by eight bells for the new year from Evgeny Komkov, the youngest at twenty seven.

New Years Day 2008.

A very quiet day with no visitors from the shore. I took a long lonesome walk to the nearest civilization, The Belle View bar at Ijmuiden where I had last imbibed three years ago when delivering the "Alice K." I had a few beers in convivial company, and a long reflective walk back again. Twenty seven days since we had arrived in St.Petersburg, and apart from my cheerful Irish engineer, there was nothing I liked about this ship. Was she jinxed?

2nd January. Two carpenters appeared to see what we required but when told that due to holidays it would take three or four days to obtain materials and do the work I dismissed them. Komkov and I found a stout lump of wood and cut it to shape to jam between my bunk and toilet bulkhead and prevent movement until the job could be done properly in Singapore. The other jobs were similarly botched up. A Rolls Royce engineer came but left saying a controls man was needed, so another day went by. On 3rd January the required technicians reported in and we had a visit from the boss, who said that Svitzer were angry and impatient at our delays and costs for which we were to blame. He sampled the Gulag soup and through Berezovskiy questioned the seamen, who confirmed they had no experience of cooking or inclination to learn as wife and mother did it at home. The boss promised to have cooks put on board from a launch as we passed Malta, or transited the Suez canal en route to Singapore. So although the five day forecast was for gales we departed Ijmuiden on 4th January, glad to put Russia and Europe behind us. I was elated, at last bound for…"Somewhere East of Suez, where a man can raise a thirst, an' there aint no ten commandments, an' the best is like the worst!"

5th and 6th January we battled our way down the North Sea, through the Dover Strait and into the Channel, with headwinds and seas rising, green seas tumbling over the bow, and spray obscuring the view from the bridge.

On 7th January we were a few miles from a French fishing vessel reported sinking. On behalf of our two tugs I spoke to the French coastguard explaining that we could do little to help as we were labouring in extreme sea conditions. They authorized us to continue on passage. Helicopters were searching for the six man crew. I believe Igor in the "Busse" was oblivious to all this drama, as he said nothing.

It took three days to cross Biscay Bay, rocking and rolling all the way. E-mails raged back and forth on the subject of cooks but the owners were adamant, no cooks would be supplied.

Gradually as we worked our way down the Iberian coast the weather improved, we changed into shorts and shirts, and generally began to enjoy life. One day a bowl of boiled eggs appeared on the messroom table, sixteen eggs to be precise, an odd number for a crew of six. After my Gulag soup I carried a mug of coffee and an egg to the bridge to relieve the watch, cracked the egg on the chartroom table, and had a mess to clear up. Later Ted said he had popped an egg into his boiler suit on his way to the engine room, and arrived there with a sticky mess in the pocket. On the plus side we were achieving a speed of eight knots with good economical fuel figures, somewhat better than the "Busse". We took special satisfaction from this as the "Busse's" Alexander frequently called our Alex. on the VHF to lecture him on how best to run the engines. This sometimes resulted in adjustments made without reference to Ted, which caused friction. We also suspected that in the "Busse" the Second Engineer had more control than the Chief. In time the Dutch office noticed the difference in the daily consumption figures I reported, and began to ask questions. This increased my workload, as did the requests for defect and deficiency lists required on a ship's maiden voyage while under guarantee. Ted kept his lists short and to the point, compared to the other who was prone to flowery imagery such as, "This engineroom must have been designed by schoolchildren!" "The bilge pump wouldn't suck the skin off a rice pudding!"

Faced with the owner's obduracy, and aware of the bad state of catering on board, the Dutch boss offered to send us cooks at his expense, so we held another conference. It was clear the seamen who produced the Gulag soup were not going to improve, and unfortunately the Russian officers were not prepared to back us against the owners who employed them. Reluctantly we decided we could not accept the generous Dutch offer, and agreed to put up with the status quo for the four or five weeks remaining. Nikolai and Ted both offered to prepare an occasional meal but I do not approve of senior personnel neglecting their own work or precious sleep to cook. Recalling Solzhenitsyn's tale of the Gulag, "One Day in the Life of Ivan Denisovich," I counselled that it was not the shortage of food or its poor quality that killed. (It was the lickers of other peoples' plates who died, of diseases contracted and compounded by their loss of self esteem.) We could and would put up with the owner's contempt for our welfare, and our health would not suffer unduly.

Ted Burke was a constant source of good humour and support. The Irish prevent us Anglo Saxons from taking ourselves too seriously, and over a can of beer or glass of wine Ted and I regaled each other with poetry and song, and "divil take these sullen Ruskys!"

The day before arrival at Port Said we allowed unrestricted use of water, recognizing that we had conserved it well and would replenish our tanks at the canal. Galley and messroom were swabbed out and everyone dhobied their clothes. On 22nd January we anchored off Port Said to await our assigned convoy. I had not made a Suez Canal transit since 1956 when I was Apprentice so suggested Joe Benneton should lead us through, and invited his advice on local conditions.

"Well of course," says Joe, "This is known as Marlboro Country meaning nothing happens without liberal dispensation of cigarettes. I reckon on fourteen cartons to get me through. Also guard against theft of anything not welded down, especially brass firehose nozzles, and the like."

January 23rd. From 0100 to 2100 was spent transiting the Suez Canal with the help or hindrance of government officials, pilots, customs, tonnage measurers, chandlers, boatmen, and others who depleted my store of Marlboro by nineteen cartons, 3,800 cigarettes.

January 24th, at anchor in Suez Bay we took diesel, fresh water, and provisions. "Svitzer Busse" required nineteen tons more diesel than us reflecting Ted's more economical operation of the engines. From the Gulf of Suez I sent an estimated time of arrival at Singapore of 19th February, a twenty six day passage.

En route we passed EL Tor in Sinai where, forty nine years before I had called for a quarantine inspection of a load of Muslim "hadjis", pilgrims we were transporting from Jiddah to Port Tewfik. And later passed El Quseir where, when I was Apprentice we loaded 10,000 tons of phosphate for Japan. I thought of shipmates dead and gone; names and faces now less real than faces in the clouds.

Because of the heat Berezovskiy had his head shaved to a white egg dome so that with black moustache and hairy chest he resembled a Turkish wrestler. Instant transformation from Ivan Petrovsky Skovar to Abdul Abulbul Amir.

On the way down the Red Sea the "Busse" suffered a major breakdown in her air conditioning system, beyond repair with the equipment available. Whereas our normal company crew would probably have continued without it, sleeping on deck if necessary, the owners' men were noisily complaining that the heat in the accommodation was intolerable. Aden and Djibouti were considered unsafe as ports of refuge, so "Busse" was directed to Salalah in Oman, and I was told to continue to Singapore. The tugs parted ways on 30th

January which I entered in my diary as a Red Letter Day! So relieved was I at ridding myself of the burden of handling all the "Busse's" correspondence.

My euphoria was short lived. On Friday 1st February at around 1600 pirates attacked.
We saw a white plastic skiff approaching fast, and sprang into action. I changed from auto to manual steering control, increased engine speed and propeller pitch to maximum, while Berezovskiy sounded the general alarm, pressed the secret button to alert a control centre in the U.K. which would activate a tracking device, and put out a "MAYDAY" call on the VHF (which nobody answered). Alexander went to the engineroom while Ted and the seamen joined us in the wheelhouse having secured the steel maindeck doors from within. We were ready to repel boarders, let battle commence!

They approached fast on the starboard quarter, five dark men, heads swathed in white rags, armed with Kalshnikovs except the man aft on the outboard engine. As they came level with our stern I turned the port thruster control 90 degrees to give our stern a three thousand horsepower lurch towards them. Just in time they veered away, circled and came again, only to be forced away once more. I was gaining in confidence that I could keep them off, but in case I actually hit and sank them I called on Ted to take pictures to prove they were armed, not innocent fishermen run down and sunk. On the next attempt they fired shots, "Crack! Crack! Crack!" We all ducked but standing up to steer I was relieved to note no broken glass. Their shots were to intimidate, not kill. Then Ted shouted that only four pirates were in the boat. Had the other boarded us? No! The bowman with boarding ladder had fallen into the sea and was swimming back to his mates. I considered running back over him, but rejected that idea as they would certainly have fired on our wheelhouse, and I was not yet mad enough to kill. They appeared to give up, and we lumbered away east with Ted tweaking the revs and pitch for top speed, about twelve knots.
Then to our dismay we saw a second boat arrive with four gunmen, and they approached simultaneously, one on each quarter. Deep down I knew we were doomed, but I was suddenly furious, and determined to smash one boat hoping the other would stop to rescue swimmers, and then perhaps overloaded and sluggish I could sink the other, or they would call off the attack. In they came, bouncing over our wake, firing sporadically, and I threw the stern violently side to side. In a welter of white water we rolled and surged, wallowed and plunged, yelling and swearing in English and Russian, excited, terrified, murderous, no time to think! Until a shout, "They're aboard!" The fight was over. I dropped the revs and pitch to zero and brought the thrusters together, stopping our tug in the water. A hush fell over the wheelhouse, and a crescendo of shots and shouts clattered up the steel stairways to the bridge.

First to appear was a short stocky one with bulging eyes who announced he was Andrew, and the hard looking middleweight beside him was "Omar, our Captain". We were to take orders only from them. Was I the Captain, and what name? I gave my first name "Colin" as the Russians were not familiar with my surname, and ever after I was "Captain Colin" in good times and bad. Others sidled into the wheelhouse and indicated with their Kalashnikovs that the Russians were to sit on the deck. Ted and I stood together listening intently to a harangue on the sad state of Somalia, with no government or public services for seventeen years. The emergence of "militias" to fund their lives through hijacking and ransoms, and assurance that unless we sabotaged their efforts we would be unharmed. But Andrew warned,

"We are Muslims! We don't afraid to die, and we don't afraid to kill! I myself have killed two men!" But I doubted he had ever killed a rabbit. Omar, on the other hand, was full of dark menace, and others were shouting and glaring wild eyed.

"They are angry because you fight them," said Andrew.

"Me fight? What with? You have the guns!" I replied indignantly.

"No, no, but you try to sink our boats!" he persisted. My answer,

"It is my duty to prevent armed robbers from boarding my ship," when translated appeared to be accepted. It puzzled them that we had no cargo or passengers, and a crew of only six.

Their first priority was to hoist aboard the skiffs so I dispatched Nikolai and the seamen, shadowed by gunmen, to deploy the crane and fetch rope for slings. The first boat being half flooded was abandoned after its engine, ammunition and assorted luggage, was transferred to the second, which already had its own outboard plus a spare, three 48HP Yamahas. With slings placed the last pirate jumped aboard the tug and signalled to hoist. Komkov complied, even when the skiff rose from the water at a crazy angle, and continued to heave until it cleared the water and the weight, all at one end, parted the sling and everything plunged to the bottom, a mile deep. A couple of cans of petrol remained floating on the placid sea. Ted and I exchanged glances thinking of Spike Milligan's character Eccles, with his catch phrase, "It's fallen in the water!" but we dared not laugh at the pirates' misfortune.

"Never mind!" says Andrew, "We didn't need that, full ahead!"

The first named destination was Caluula, seventy miles away on the Somali coast, which they said they had left two hours before. Ted and I were determined to go at our economical speed of eight knots, and when they protested at the slowness Ted scrolled through the monitor until he found red lines indicating high temperatures, high pressures, so we remained slow. On the understanding that I would be shot if tricks were played the crew were permitted to leave the bridge for toilet calls, coffee and snacks. On return they reported that the cabins were being ransacked for cash and valuables, especially anything electronic which could be used for communication with the outside world. Several times Omar stabbed a finger at the chart indicating a new destination, away from Caluula, to Cape Guardafui, then towards Hafun, and on down Somalia's east coast. When I enquired politely through Andrew where our ultimate location might be I was advised insolently to just follow Omar's orders. We continued our normal six hour watches, making standard log book entries, keeping as much control as possible.

When my turn came to sleep I found the cabin a shambles of clothes, papers, books, my briefcase looted of personal cash plus a substantial sum of Company's money, the toilet full of faeces, and a pirate in my bunk. Rudely awakened, he bolted out the door.

During my next watch we encountered stronger monsoon wind, with consequent rolling. A pirate was sea sick down the flight of wheelhouse stairs and I told Kimochkin to clean it up. His attitude was that the pirate should do it himself, but my will prevailed.

Acting as my eyes and ears Ted reported that the Russians were considering "jumping" three pirates for their weapons, and shooting the other six. I strongly vetoed this desperate plan, and spoke to Berezovskiy. I explained that none of us knew how we would get through this difficult period, but our best ploy was to comply with the wishes of the gunmen, not to provoke them into violence, but to treat them with reserve, even respect, and hope that we would be treated likewise. We would need their cooperation in the conserving of provisions, especially water, the maintaining of hygiene, indeed the preservation of the ship for future service, and they clearly needed us to operate the ship. I was confident that a ransom would eventually be paid for our release. Berezovskiy at once asserted that Putin would not pay one rouble for a Russian life. Fortunately it would not be up to Putin. Most importantly I expected Nikolai, as Mate, to assist me in controlling the Russians, all owner's men, not Redwise.

I asked Ted if he knew that Kimochkin translated as Curmudgeon, and he replied,
"Is that so Colin? The breadth of your knowledge never ceases to amaze me!"

This first night passed with our little tug proceeding without lights down the east coast of Somalia. As a soldier Omar urged us in close to the breakers where he felt comfortable, smelling the sand. Berezovskiy and I preferred to stay outside the 10 metre sounding line, fearing isolated dangers, rocks or wrecks which could cripple our thrusters. Somali coastal lights are unlit as no one pays the lighthouse keepers. We ran off the edge of our paper chart, not having made provision for a deviation along these shores.

Henceforth I was obliged to rely on the electronic charts Berezovskiy had bought in some St.Petersburg backstreet, a complete world set for £100, highly illegal and years out of date. The owners had installed the instrument to display electronic charts but had not supplied charts. All this was noted in the Official Log Book. Piracy notwithstanding a ship must be operated as closely as possible in compliance with the law, and continuity in her records must be maintained.

On this day, Saturday the 2nd February 2008, there was a noticeable thaw in pirate crew relations. We were allowed more freedom to move about the ship, and I got permission for the two seamen to clean the accommodation. Better to be working than brooding. Berezovskiy was in a bad way, depressed and morose. Lichkunov reported that after his watch he had swallowed a lot of pills and taken to his bunk without a word, so I left him sleeping for part of his next watch. Ted asserted his authority over the engine room and his right to make checks, to transfer oils, change filters, and other routines. He reported that though gunmen always escorted him there and back they invariably stayed on the top landing, not liking to descend among the hot noisy machinery. An observation he later put to good use.

Andrew dropped the pretence of an English name and became Sancha to all. He, together with a quiet pleasant fellow called Ahmed, in apologetic manner explained why they had become pirates, or militia as they preferred. For lack of government, and faced with the plundering of their fisheries by foreigners, and dumping of toxic waste in their seas, they had created a sort of coastguard of two hundred men operating in teams of ten. At first they had confiscated fish catches but then, as the big foreign fishing ships began arming themselves, they found it easier to take passing merchant ships to hold to ransom.

Ted listened closely, nodding in agreement, and encouraging them with questions, but suddenly I saw Omar, excluded from this cosy chat by his lack of English, glaring fiercely under knotted brows, like a bull about to explode into violent action. I stepped back, took up the binoculars and pretended an interest in something ashore, and Omar stopped pawing the ground. Without a common language I would need to work hard to establish a good relationship with this formidable opponent, but I had a lot to gain, or lose. I would let Ted get close to the talkers and learn what he could, while I kept my distance, maintaining my dignity, as Master of the ship.

When Berezovskiy eventually awoke and took over the bridge watch I gratefully fell into my bunk for a deep sleep, leaving my spectacles, knife, and watch, on a small shelf by my head. To my disgust when I awoke the watch and knife were missing. On the bridge I complained about this theft and Ahmed promptly went to investigate. He soon returned with the watch and advised,

"Captain, you must be careful, some of these men are t'ieves!"

Sunday 3rd February. At 0130 we put down the starboard anchor with five shackles of cable in 10 metres, eight cables from the shore close to the fishing village of Eyl. Nearby was a Singapore fishing vessel which the pirates proudly described as another of "theirs", held to ransom.

At breakfast I asked each crewmember in turn whether they were on any prescribed medicine, which, if it ran out before our release could present a problem. All replied in the negative.

At 0845 I was allowed to speak on the satellite telephone to the boss in Holland. I confirmed what he already knew through following the tracking device that we had been highjacked, that we were all well, and before the 'phone was grabbed away from me I described the pirates as plain robbers, not political or religious fanatics. He gave me a name, David Green, and a Copenhagen telephone number which should be my exclusive conduit for information. On a personal level he told me my lifelong friend Keith Harding was with my wife Barbara. That was a tremendous comfort given that Keith had a military background enabling him to give her sound and reliable advice, and be able to liaise with the Foreign Office and any other authorities which might get involved. I could safely concentrate on my job.

At 1045 I was authorized to send emails to the Owners in Copenhagen, with copies to the future operators in Sakhalin, and my Dutch boss. These related that nine pirates had captured the ship and were demanding US$2.5 million for our release, and if this was not agreed within three days they would shoot the crew and keep the ship.

I was later told these emails did not get through but I don't believe it.

Ahmed asked me for a shirt, opening a colourful jacket of Ted's to reveal a bare chest. He said all his clothes had gone down with the boat when the sling carried away. I gave him a Company T- shirt.

From Eyl some of the ubiquitous white skiffs came off with more armed pirates plus food for them mostly consisting of bundles of narcotic weed. This stringy weed called Qat, or Khat, is evidently imported from Kenya where it grows up in the hills at the same altitude as tea. Muslims are denied alcohol but this mild narcotic is permitted and appears to be a national addiction in Somalia. I anxiously observed its effect, and was relieved to see it made them mellow rather than aggressive, though you can never take for granted the mood of anyone drugged up.

Our garrison of nine pirates was augmented from the shore to a total of twenty or twenty five. The figure uncertain as they came and went in a random manner. When I asked where all this lot would sleep and how we were to feed them I was told to mind my own business. The newcomers included one Abdul Azziz whom we nicknamed the "mullah". He was young with a fluffy black beard, probably never cut, a small white cap, wire rimmed spectacles, long white robe, and leather sandals, and he did the ritual praying for all hands. He seldom spoke but when he did his English was quite good, slow and deliberate, without humour. He took his turn at guard duty with a kalashnikov.

Before the pirates arrived Ted had rigged a small hose to collect the air conditioning condensate water into wheelie bins on the maindeck. This was to supplement our fresh water tankage, and initially we used it only to flush the toilets, but now with greatly increased "crew" we also used it for laundry and cooking. I explained this need for water economy to Omar and he agreed to cooperate. He chose to use my toilet, and as he chose not to flush it I was able to keep an eye on his state of health through observation of the colour and consistency of his stools, satisfactory at that time. He also wore my gym shoes, but the pirates all stubbed out their fag ends with their bare feet, from which I inferred that shoes, when worn, were merely a fashion accessory or status symbol. The young pirate cook wore my Cotton Traders tracksuit bottoms, but as he was so much better at cooking than our Russian seamen I let that pass.

At this anchorage Ted used a two inch hook baited with rotten prawns to catch his first fish. It was long and slimy with bites out of it, but an encouraging start.

83

In the early evening a panic ran through the Somalis and we were all hastily gathered together in the wheelhouse. A warship had approached, at first assumed to be Somali government. There was much running in circles and shouting, especially a little guy we called "Sammy" because of his resemblance to Sammy Davis Junior. Sammy yelled at me "Soldiers of America, go 'way! Go 'way! You speak!" indicating the VHF telephone, "Soldiers of America, Go 'way!" Out of all this chaos some kind of order was imposed by Captain Omar, with men stationed fore and aft and on top the wheelhouse with Kalashnikovs, RPGs (rocket propelled grenades), and a machinegun on a tripod. But the strange warship backed off and pirates and hostages gradually relaxed. Omar and Sancha agreed my request to 'phone David Green in Copenhagen and I repeated the ransom terms. Green undertook to commence gathering together some money and asked me to provide in due course a name, telephone number and bank account details of a middleman presumed to be in Djibouti.

Suddenly at 2100 Omar sent us all off to bed.

Monday 4th February.
I was washed and shaved by 0500 and went to the bridge. I had to convince Omar that the radar showed no other ships near us, but he did not know I was operating the radar on very close range. At 0700 I got Kimochkin out of bed to clean up the mess of khat leaves and stalks scattered everywhere, and Komkov to sort out the galley and fix breakfast. The Somalis mostly slept late after hours on the weed. When I asked Ahmed if any real food had come aboard he replied,
"This African food." So it appears they can live on the weed.
The warship appeared again at a distance and I was ordered to get the anchor up and proceed down the coast, "Maybe ten hours!" But at 1130 Omar suddenly waved me in towards a headland marked Ras El Chiel where we put the port anchor down in 12 metres. This was an exposed position where we pitched and plunged in the strong monsoon and I steadily put out more chain until we finally lay with both anchors on the bottom with five shots of cable each side. At midday they killed and ate a goat procured at Eyl and showed me a second one tethered on the after deck which was for the crew.

I made my promised 'phone call to David Green in Copenhagen but it was a waste of time as the pirates had no bank accounts or intermediaries to receive the cash. They now insisted on cash on board, but I patiently explained that no man from Denmark could fly into Somalia with suitcases of dollars, come trotting over the desert on donkey or camel, and then a skiff out to us, without being robbed along the way. Then the shipowner would have lost his money and still be deprived of his ship.

Around 1700 Ahmed said peevishly,
"Captain, your goat still live!" I explained that none of my men wanted to kill the little goat, but he insisted, "Goat must die!"
So not wishing to appear ungrateful I agreed to personally kill it assisted by a pirate. A tall skinny one came with me to the galley and selected the longest knife from the rack and with a flick of the wrist severed the tether, tipped the little goat on his back and indicated that I should hold the four small feet together in one hand. This done he carefully cut the throat half way through and retired to sit on a winch and roll a cigarette while I held the struggling bleating animal as its life blood ebbed away into the scuppers. When it ceased moving my pirate sliced off the head and tossed it overboard, and then expertly skinned and gutted it. The guts went overside then in turn he held up heart, liver, and kidneys, and as I shook my head they also went into the oggin. Finally he cut the little carcase in two and we placed them in plastic bags in the freezer on deck. A few days later Ted quietly reported that they had eaten our little goat.

Later that evening, mellow with weed, they handed me a mobile phone with six dollars credit on it and said I should 'phone my wife. Barbara was delighted to hear me, said that Keith and a policeman were with her, and she had been speaking to Ted's wife Doreen. I've since been told this call was recorded and my largely cheerful remarks were well received, and even amazed the policeman. When I judged I'd had enough time the pirates waved me on. All this augured well.
Another mobile burst into song. Sancha picked it up,
"What? CNN? No news!"

Thus ended quite an eventful day.

5th February, Tuesday.

During the night the anchors dragged and I picked them up and re-anchored. It really was an unsuitable spot which Omar had chosen. At 0800 I again shifted and logged the new latitude as 07 13.4N.
At 1400 I phoned David Green and managed to give him some information on our abductors, and their general incompetence.

The warship reappeared and came close causing consternation. We were all herded together in the wheelhouse to be human shields in case of attack. I was manhandled and told to inform the warship that unless they cleared off we would all die. As expected the warship ignored the threats and stayed close. It was then discovered to be American not Somali. I believe the photograph subsequently given me by USNS Carney was taken here as it showed the tug pitching heavily against a cliffy rockbound coast, unlike the background of other pictures taken at Gabbac.

This American warship, which referred to itself as "coalition" put out a routine message on the VHF. It said they would not permit resupply from the shore, and urged the pirates to leave the ship and hostages unharmed, and depart without bloodshed on either side. The Americans did not respond to questions, threats, or requests, and at that point I admired their technique. It appeared very professional, gathering snippets of information from every interchange but giving nothing away themselves. They appeared to be dictating and the pirates responding, and I got the impression the pirates knew they were outclassed.

6th February.

At anchor with five shackles on each and still dragging. Suddenly at 0430 with a loud bang we lost the port anchor which rattled and roared out through the hawsepipe.
We naturally assumed the port anchor had got a grip on the bottom and suddenly having the full weight of the ship had parted the cable. But later in Salalah when we inspected the chain locker we found that the system of securing the bitter end was in the open position. Berezovskiy had said that during seatrials the port anchor had been damaged and removed for repair, and now it was apparent that it had never been properly resecured to the chain locker bulkhead. Dereliction of duty by the shipyard and the Mate, Berezovskiy, who should have checked.

Just before dawn when the Mate and Kimochkin were attending to the anchor, Ted and Alexander were in the engine room, and just Komkov and me in the wheelhouse with Omar and a few gunmen, I got to thinking that he and I were at the height of our careers. I would never face a more difficult situation, needing all my experience to get us out of this predicament unscathed, and Omar had never taken such a valuable prize. But by the end of the day, with the warship threatening one of us could be dead. So I turned to him and said that he had shown himself to be a good commander and worthy adversary, and held out my hand. He extended his long thin brown fingers and we shook hands. As I turned away he asked the gunmen what that was all about, but none could enlighten him. It was a bit Hollywood theatrical but I hoped he could not so easily shoot me after that.

Now with only one anchor I had to point out to Omar that we could not take the risk of losing it and leaving ourselves with nothing. That would necessitate operating the engines constantly and eventually running out of diesel. I managed to persuade him to take my advice and move into a decent sheltered anchorage where our sole anchor would suffice. As the monsoon wind appeared stronger to the south and weaker north I recommended going back north. He clearly resented relinquishing control to me but in the end common sense prevailed and we steamed north. Off Eyl the weather was still rough so taking advantage of Omar's temporary absence from the bridge I pressed on up the coast, escorted by the warship putting out its routine message.

About fourteen miles north of Eyl there was a deep fracture in the coastal plateau, a wadi, generally dry but occasionally discharging fresh water into the sea. According to the electronic chart a delta of mud had built up over millenia, extending seaward from the mouth of the wadi, or arroyo as they call it elsewhere. Omar appeared just as I was shaping my approach, in a foul mood as I had bypassed Eyl but now impatient to get the anchor down. I sent Nikolai and old Pyotr to the foredeck to drop the hook on my signal, and crept in watching soundings and the breakers along the shore. Light was fading and Omar's temper rising. He began shouting "Go hon! Go hon!" and waving his left hand while cradling his gun with the right. Suddenly he reached over and cuffed the back of my head, "smack!" In one movement I put the thrusters together stepped back a pace crossed my arms and swore at him.
"If you hit me you bastard the fucking ship goes nowhere!" He couldn't understand the words but the import of what I said must have been obvious. For long seconds we glared at each other, and then he resumed yelling "Go hon!" without the blows. I grasped the controls and crept in until I finally signalled the dropping of the anchor. It was off the village of Gabbac (the C is silent), and there we stayed for the next forty days. But in the interim their boat's painter had got under our counter and been chopped up, allowing the boat to drift away. Our rescue boat was quickly craned overside and a couple of pirates took it away and retrieved their boat. It had been a trying day. I drank my last bottle of beer and found the hidden bottle of wine missing.

At 2200 Ahmed advised me to go to bed as Omar was drunk and looking for trouble, so I did and locked the door.

7th February, Thursday.

Up at 0230 to check the position, which was good. Spoke briefly to Nikolai on watch. Up again at 0600 washed and shaved and took a clean shirt.

Mid morning Omar not liking us all talking together sent us off to individual cabins.
In 1400 routine phone call to David Green he made a number of points, principally that the warship was not under Svitzer's control. They wanted a quick and peaceful end without bloodshed, and could deliver US$258,000 anywhere, such as Dubai or Kenya. When this message was translated and digested the pirates were hopping mad and angrily re-demanded US$2.5 million with the new threat that if it was not agreed by tomorrow they would run the ship ashore and kill us all. Meanwhile we were all confined to individual cabins. I reflected that if death was to come I would try to face it calmly, not begging for mercy or praying to god in whom I have no belief, standing up, without a blindfold. John Steinbeck's words came to mind.

"It seems good to mark and to remember for a little while the place where a man died. This is his one whole lonely act in all his life. In every other thing, even in his birth, he is bound close to others, but the moment of his dying is his own."

That said, I would have to face the gunman with courage and dignity. But I would not spit in his eye, for which he might beat or torture me, and I wouldn't want to die in pain.

Ted and I also promised to visit each other's families if one or the other survived.

At 1800 I was summoned to the bridge and sat in my seat as the warship approached to within 7 cables of us. I didn't look at her, feigning indifference, but I watched on the radar screen. She pulled abeam and there were flashes as of a camera. Then she moved away to three miles and I was released.

8th February.
The day started with a good wash and shave. Good strong sweet Somali tea urged upon me by "Sammy Davis Junior" whose real name was Fife. This man and Ahmed had both served in the proper coastguard when there was a government, and this made them a little more civilized with reasonable English. From them I learned that the little white building with red tiled roof on the headland near the village of round thatched huts, was a British field hospital in WWll. The British had fought hereabouts and forced the Italians to retreat

to Mogadishu. The areas formerly under British protectorate were now better than the formerly Italian parts. Ahmed's father and Omar's had fought together for the British in Kenya, which I presumed to be against the Mau Mau.

I had a useful chat with Ted. We agreed that while not helping the pirates we would stop short of sabotage which if discovered would be counter productive. The night, between two and four was the best time for smuggling away tins of food. I had a half jar of honey in my waste basket under a lot of rubbish. One developed a sort of prison mentality getting a thrill out of deceiving the guards, winning minor points. But I felt the need to restrain Ted as he proposed various dodgy schemes. In a few days we would make an incinerator out of an old oil drum to burn up the rubbish, mainly packaging. It would boost morale by giving the boys something to do. The general truculence and pessimism of the Russians was a problem which idleness would exacerbate.

This morning Burke and I were called to the bridge to sit there as some action took place. Two boats approached with stores. The frigate opened fire with shells skimming the water. One boat turned back but the other got through with sacks of Turkish spaghetti, flour, coca-cola, 7-up, cigarettes, and khat. This boat was fired on as it returned to the beach but was not hit. I found a pirate had left shorts and pants on my bathroom deck. He had messed right through them and when I picked them up to throw them out a large coin fell on the deck. "Ah! A doubloon!" says I. But no, it was a seven sided Australian fifty pence piece.

Also arriving with this stores boat was a new interpreter who introduced himself thus.
"I am Mohammad Abdul Ali. I am a respectable schoolmaster not one of these bandits! They have force-ed me to work for them as a solicitor and interpreter to help obtain the money and your release. I do not have much time, my students need me. I am known as Gele because of this." And he opened his mouth showing all centre top teeth missing, so Gele must mean "gappy".
I shook hands and asked him how much they would pay him, to which he promptly replied five thousand dollars. I pointed out that this made him a pirate like the rest and when caught he would be hanged alongside the others. He didn't like that.

At the daily 'phone call Gele did all the talking to impress pirates and crew alike with his fluency. He emphasised that 2.5 million dollars was the "lastest" figure, or they would start killing the crew beginning with the captain.

The old interpreter Andrew/Sancha had apparently fallen foul of Omar. Ted reported him being dragged out of the winchroom where he had spent the night. He had a damaged shoulder but was thrown onto the deck in the sun, and chained by a wrist. The short chain used for securing barrels did not allow the man any freedom to turn over, so Ted fetched a longer chain from the engine room and placed it near the prisoner but there was no move to substitute it. In fact when Ted later collected a bucket of water to flush his toilet he was urged to chuck it over the unfortunate Sancha, but declined. Sancha had appeared to be a crony of Omar, but he was a bit cocky so perhaps had overstepped the mark and had to be taught a lesson.

On the bridge that evening the usual senior pirates and Omar were joined by Gele, who said,
"Captain Omar asks me to find out what things you want," and prepared to make a list. I started with milk, tinned or powdered, fruit and vegetables, and so on. Gele said we could take the ship to another region where fruit and veg were more freely available, but I preferred this safe anchorage to taking our chances elsewhere.
Finally, feeling goodwill in the air I told this solicitor/translator that Omar had treated us with respect, which we appreciated. When this was relayed the response was,
"If no faults respectance will continue."
Gele, eager to practice his English told us he was 29 years old, unmarried, and ran a school for 150 fee paying students. He had been visiting his grandmother when pirates had intercepted him and "force-ed" him to come and help them. An assistant was running the school in his absence but he could not stay long. He urged me to persuade the owners to increase their offer. I explained that I worked for the Dutch delivery Company, not the Danish owners and had never previously heard of David Green, meaning I had very little influence in the matter. This also accorded with my policy of sitting on the fence, occupying the middle ground as merely the telephone operator, and I intended Gele to convey this information to Omar.

To end the day Ted produced the best meal we had had since St. Petersburg, a stir fry based upon Turkish noodles with chicken, red and green peppers and garlic.

9th February, Saturday.

A tall powerfully built pirate came complaining of toothache and showed us a lower molar which had split into its four component parts with a black central hole. I delegated Ted to attend to this assisted by Nikolai with the Russian medical kit. Afterwards we referred to this character as "The Tooth".

"Sammy Davis Junior" gave me the galley kettle today saying they would make their own tea in a pan. So I set up an old Marlboro box on my cabin desk with tea, coffee, creamer, plastic cups, and the kettle beside, for when I was entertaining. I marked the box, "Cantina, all money taken!" The box also conveniently hid the unmarked red button, partner to the one on the bridge used for alerting the world to piracy attack. I feared the school teacher being a nosey type might ask its purpose.

In the evening Burke and I were told to send email greetings to our wives, but to include the threats; supervised by Gele. This was my message.

Hi Barbara, we are all well and Ted is a great help with food and morale, we as ever optimistic, but this is the message from our captors-
Our situation is in danger. If the company rejects the demands of the militia for two and a half million us dollars then we shall kill all crew. This will be Company's responsibility, not ours.
With all our love, you have been a wonderful wife, Colin.
This militia is greeting you, your husband will be released without condition if the company allows our demands.

10th February, Sunday.

A boat came off today with five gallons of camel milk of which I was given a large glass to sample and found it very tasty. Ted tried it but the Russians declined. A five litre bottle was put in the fridge for our use, and we were given a large tin of Australian milk powder.

The daily routine call to David Green produced no fresh news on the money situation, but he said our emails had upset our families and would henceforth be blocked to avoid any future distress.

At 1600 I was called to the bridge to protest to warship 64 firing at our supply boat. The firing continued all evening with splashes on the sea and puffs of sand along the shore. This persisted during darkness with bright lights and tracer shots. At one time the teacher fell to his knees and prayed. These attempts at preventing our resupply were actually futile. There were about twenty identical white skiffs drawn up along the beach. Most of them in use by the village fishermen to tend their nets and lobster pots, but occasionally one of these innocent looking craft would creep along until hidden from the warship's view, behind us, and then streak out to us with the goods. The warship was too deep to come closer to us anchored in shallow water. We crew were kept cooped up in the wheelhouse all night, until the situation eased at dawn.

11th February.

Cornflakes and camel's milk for breakfast.

Today David Green upped the offer to US$427,000 but this was rejected out of hand.
Lots more gunfire this day caused high tension and bad temper among the pirates. I was forced to re anchor even closer to the breakers. Without explanation we were all sent to our cabins at 2100 with orders to leave lights on and doors open, no conversing between us, and twenty minute patrols would ensure our compliance. I stayed awake to observe the efficiency of these patrols and only noticed two checks before midnight.

This is an appropriate time to step back from my diary notes for a recapitulation.

Up to this time we had been treated reasonably well and allowed the use of our cabins, bathrooms, galley, and messroom. Movement within the accommodation was pretty much unrestricted, and Ted and Alex could check the Engine Room, freezers, fridges, air conditioning equipment etc.
Ted and I still had a few bottles of beer which we regularly shared before lunch, or dinner, though the schoolteacher sometimes hung around, curious as to what we were saying. Among the innocent chats we began to plan some positive action towards our release. The Jews who survived the holocaust are sometimes criticised for the way so many of their race went meekly into the gas chambers. Ted Burke and I felt we should not just sit and wait for a ransom to be paid. The plan we settled on was to black out the ship, hide ourselves in the stern, behind barricaded watertight doors, and thus leave the way clear for American marines to attack, kill or frighten off the pirates, and free us and the ship. Success depended upon me alerting the Americans to this plan, and we spent some time working on coded messages for me to slip into my daily contact with David Green in Copenhagen. We assumed that he would not be alone in the office, and my speech would be recorded and analysed. Some of Ted's coded messages requiring a knowledge of Irish history,

Hollywood films, and baseball players, had me completely baffled, so in the end I opted for almost plain language. As I recall it went something like this :-

11th Feb. **Before discussing the ransom I would like to say how it comforts us to know that all parties have our welfare at heart. Svitzer say our lives are their main concern; the warship says their main interest is safeguarding the lives of the hostages; the militia promise us we will not be harmed if the ransom demands are met.** Up to now my delivery had been slow and clear enough for the teacher to translate and nods from pirates showed they were following. But now I speeded up, guessing that the teacher would find it harder but would not admit that his English was inadequate. I concluded, **and as Master I promise to protect the lives of the crew, if something nasty like a blackout should occur the crew will be tucked away safe behind steel doors come what may!**

I managed to gabble it all out without interference, and was well pleased. Ted declared it perfect, assuring me that in replays in Copenhagen the key words "blackout" "steel doors" and "safe come what may" would stand out, and the Americans would be ready to attack when our lights went out. I think Ted has seen too many movies.

As this plan evolved we outlined it to the Russians who approved in principle, never having much faith in help from elsewhere. Ted and Alex, taking advantage of the pirates' reluctance to go down into the engine room, removed unseen the starting switches of the emergency lighting, and assembled a few 5 litre bottles of water in the stern compartment.
Ted was really enthused and tried to elaborate on the plan. He suggested we fit keys to all doors to lock them on our way to the engine room and delay pursuit.
"No Ted!" said I. Seeing him pottering about with keys would have alerted the pirates to the anomaly that we prisoners held the keys, and not the gaolers.

One armed man always slept in the messroom and Ted wanted at least to be able to reach in and close and lock that door in passing.
"No Ted!" He might have been just dozing and Ted's action would certainly have alarmed him and made him jump up and probably fire his gun.
On the way to the engine room Ted wanted to put a pan of diesel on the galley stove and close and lock the door just before it boiled over.
"No Ted!" He could easily have been caught in one of these non essential sideshows and be prevented from joining the rest of us in our sanctuary. Just one man on the outside to be tortured would have wrecked our plan.

I felt like the chairman of the escape committee at Colditz vetting harebrained ideas.

On 11th February the warship fired a lot of shots at the supply boats and appeared to hit the beach and cliffs, as well as firing tracer bullets, and dropping bright lights on top of the cliffs apparently with parachutes attached. Some people were injured or killed. The pirates said they had been attacked by "government" soldiers ashore, had suffered one man injured, and killed two soldiers. The warship officer said he had seen a casualty being carried along the beach by stretcher, and asked me if I had any information on the condition of that person.

I have since seen this Reuters report.:-
XXX

13th February 2008. Puntland troops trade fire with Somali pirates. This morning the pirates opened fire at our troops as they were trying to use force to release the ship," said Puntland's minister for petrol and mineral resources, Hassan Osman Mohammad.

The fighting broke out as troops on land fired at pirates docked nearby as they wait to have supplies of food and weapons taken to them by accomplices in smaller boats, he said.

"We understand that our troops and the pirates exchanged gunfire killing one civilian in the nearby village and wounding one of our troops," he told Reuters by telephone.

He said the pirates had used long-range arms, striking a few houses in a nearby fishing village.

XXX

The pirates told me to tell the Americans that their efforts to stop us being resupplied were not working (this was obvious) but because of their firing the local fishermen were afraid to come out to tend their nets, or dive for lobsters, and this was causing hardship to the local community. I passed this message on and the Americans agreed to reduce the harassment.

A few words about the place Gabbac off which we were anchored. For many miles the shoreline consisted of a narrow beach of sand with a few scrubby bushes and rocks backed by steep cliffs rising to 500 to 600 feet, the edge of a desert plateau.

Opposite us was a deep gorge or canyon cut over centuries by an occasional watercourse, a wadi or arroyo winding back in great sweeping curves. The water, when it occasionally flowed appeared to end in a fresh water lake, with no obvious exit to the sea. Pirates' and fishermen's boats, all the same model, six metre plastic, were drawn up on the sandbar between the sea and the shallow lake. Around and beyond the lake was some vegetation, and we occasionally saw camels and goats and one or two horses and a cow. On the right of the wadi on slopes rising to the plateau were about eight orange tents, the pirates' camp. At night all this was in darkness apart from the odd oil lamp early in the evening. One could occasionally see females at or near these tents. Our pirates spoke constantly to this camp calling, "Gabba, gabba, gabba, budda". Gabbac being the name of the village up on the cliff and budda meaning "at sea" or "offshore" Very often the voice answering was female.

A path to the right of this encampment led up to the plateau where could be seen a few round huts made of sticks and thatched. Also the white building with red tiled roof said to be a former hospital but no longer manned. Two refrigerated trucks stood there, and we were told the locals dive for lobsters and put the tails in a truck until it is full when it is driven to Bosaaso for export.

All the time we were there a motorised dhow would be anchored just north of us and closer to the shore. This was said to be a Yemeni boat come to buy the local fish. When one was filled and departed another soon arrived. On one occasion the captain and engineer of one of these Yemeni boats paid us a social call. Over a cup of sweet Somali tea we attempted to converse and they were delighted when I used one of my very few Arabic words, "nakhoda" meaning Captain. Just a few words in a foreign language go a long way.

I have since seen some video footage of the village behind the cliffs taken by Valery Du Pont a very attractive French journalist. She had actually visited the area while we were there, accompanied by a Puntland government official from Garoowe with heavy military escort. The Minister was filmed talking to or arguing with local headmen. Looking at Arabs speaking I can never tell their mood as they appear to shout, with heads moving like yapping dogs, gesticulating, and repeating.

To resume the narrative.

11th February 2350

Not allowed to talk to Ted but exchanged a few notes with him, tightly folded and thrown across the alleyway when chance permitted. We agreed to put our plan into operation now, before further restrictions or erosion of our freedom made it more difficult.

Accordingly when Ted relieved Alex in the engine room at midnight he was to keep him there. When I relieved Nikolai on the bridge at midnight I was to mutter to him to collect the two seamen and the three of them to descend to the engine room via the forward escape hatch situated in their accommodation. I was then to find some reason to leave the bridge, and go to the engine room through the same hatch.

Before leaving my cabin I put down the bathroom deadlight so that from the outside no one could see if I was there. I locked the bathroom door with a key, put my wrist watch in my pocket and went to the bridge. The stairway led first to a small deck with a long desk and a few instruments, Navtex, GPS, computer linked to a satellite phone and printer/fax machine, our portable Dutch Satcom C, and a chair to sit and operate the above. Nikolai was standing at the chart table on the bridge proper, just four steps up. Fat Sancha was sitting in the "Captain's chair" and Captain Omar was lying on the deck wrapped in a blanket with his gun beside him. He opened an eye and acknowledged me sleepily.

Nikolai showed me his log entries, made a few remarks about the watch, and I nudged him and told him to go below and be ready. I had also told Ted to cause the blackout either when I appeared in the engine room or at 0015, whichever came first. I hoped at least to get away from the bridge in the confusion following lights out.

Nikolai left the bridge. Sancha heaved himself out of the chair for me to sit, but I said I would check something on the lower bridge and sit on the other chair, so Sancha slumped back in his seat. After a pause by the satcom I started down the stairs, Sancha shouted "Hey! Where you go?" Holding up my wrist I replied,

"Forgot my watch," and away I went. Quickly down the bridge stairs, quickly down the accommodation stairs and met Nikolai and the two seamen at the bottom. We all bundled ourselves down through the escape hatch with the Russians locking two doors behind us and Kimochkin closing the escape hatch and lashing the securing dogs with rope before joining us. Reaching the engine room I shouted to Ted to blackout, we were all there.

Ted and Alexander closed the relevant fuel valves to starve the generator, made the spare generator and the emergency one inoperative, and as the lights dimmed poured oil over the engine room stairs and tied a trip rope across the bottom step. Ted would have his little sideshow. Then we all entered the hydraulic room towards the stern, closed the watertight door and tied the securing dogs with rope hoping to prevent pursuers from opening it from the other side. Time to laugh, congratulate ourselves, and take stock. All had gone well, in fact better than one could have hoped. My departure from the bridge had been easy. We had several 5 litre bottles of drinking water, and the Russians had some cigarettes. We enjoyed a rare sense of comradeship.

We chuckled as we thought of the confusion and panic among the pirates. Although some bridge and accommodation lighting would come on powered by emergency batteries, we were confident the engine room was in total darkness, and the absolute silence would be unnerving. We pictured the pirates coming down the stairs, slipping on the oil, falling, breaking arms legs or necks, and accidentally shooting each other. But we did not know that one emergency light did come on providing important illumination. The shipyard, when placing red blobs to indicate emergency lights had missed one. Damn that St. Petersburg shipyard.

To our consternation within an hour there was banging on the other side of our door, just inches away from us. We hastened back through the next WT door into the thrusters compartment. Closed that door and put a substantial bolt through the eyes welded to door and frame to take a padlock, and again screwed the dogs up tight and lashed them with rope. On the port side aft a ladder led up to an escape hatch which the engineers had already closed and bowsed downwards with a chainblock. Surely they could not enter there. Non pasaran! As they say in Spain.

We imagined the American marines blacking their faces, checking weapons, and preparing to launch rubber boats and helicopters. We only had to hold out for a few hours and the ship would be ours again. Just like in the movies a voice would call out
"Any limeys aboard? You can come out now, the Marines are here!" God bless America.

To our great alarm the pirates broke through the first door soon after one o'clock and began attacking the second door, our last barrier. Alex unbolted the hatch in the bulkhead behind us which was the Aft Peak salt water ballast tank. Ted chose to descend to a small space under the thrusters and coil himself down there. The four Russians and I entered the tank, and reversed the plate so that we had the handles on the inside to pull the plate tightly over the studs and secure it with iron bars through the handles. It was of course utterly pitch black in the tank, but someone thrust a torch into my hand. The tank was constructed as follows. The forward boundary of the tank was a bulkhead about forty feet wide, about twelve feet high in the centre, reducing out towards the ship sides to about seven feet. The

The stern of the ship formed the aft part of the tank, straight for perhaps three quarters of its length and then curving round the corners. Forward bulkhead and stern were connected by three vertical bulkheads pierced by lightening holes which gave crawl through access to the tank's extremities. Within the tank there were various flanges, ribs or frames, tie plates, vertical "floors," all to give strength to the tank which, like the bow at the other end take the forces imposed by pitching in a seaway. The tank contained about four feet of sea water ballast, but as the ship rolled constantly in the north east monsoon wind the water was never still. It rushed furiously from side to side roaring and crashing through the bulkheads which impeded its flow, and rose sometimes to perhaps six feet in the wings. The noise of rushing water made conversation impossible except in short snatches when it paused before gushing back the other way. Like hunted animals we retreated to the corner furthest from our point of entry, the port wing. There we found wide horizontal flanges to sit on between deep frames with the water level varying from ankle to waist deep. To avoid cramps we sometimes stood with heads bent under the deckhead, and did exercises, bending and stretching, and pulling and pushing against the surrounding steelwork. The Russians smoked until either all fags were used up or got wet. This made the air foul and I knew we had sealed the solitary air vent with canvas and tape to prevent sea entering the tank in rough weather when the aft deck was sometimes submerged. I occasionally switched on the torch to check the time.

So there we sat or stood, each alone with his thoughts in total darkness, isolated by the sound of roaring water, and straining to hear machinegun fire, grenades, rockets and so on, the prelude to our release.

Instead we heard the erratic cacophony of steel on steel, ringing and smashing against the escape hatch, near our heads on the port quarter of the tug. Such a sustained assault could not fail to find a weakness I feared, thinking of my old friend Captain Peter Welch's words, "With a lever long enough, and a fulcrum strong enough, you could move the world!" I wondered if they might remove the escape hatch trunking altogether by firing an RPG at it. Not being familiar with the weapon I didn't know if the blast would blow away just the hatch or a piece of the stern as well, with us in it.

Passing around the water bottles was a companionable thing to do though it led to frequent peeing through my trousers, to add to the ballast.

Where were the marines? Their storming arrival would surely occur before the pirates got through to us to use us as human shields and thwart the rescue bid. Come on Yankee Doodle where are you? I pleaded.

I did allow myself to contemplate emerging into the daylight a hero, cameras flashing, black faced marines hugging, bourbon by the pint. I could see the headlines, "Ancient British mariner defies the odds to bring out his crew alive." Asked if the surviving pirates, lined up against a bulkhead should be spared I would reply, "No, fire and be damned! Who lives by the sword dies by the sword!" Such vanity deserved its come -upance.

By 1600 I had concluded that the marines were not coming, there would be no attack, no rescue, we must give ourselves up, but with what consequences? The others had a right to a say in any surrender. I asked Nikolai's opinion. He replied that we had all suffered many hours of discomfort and should perhaps hold out a bit longer, until 1800 at least. It seemed a shame that our sacrifice had been in vain. I agreed.

However I switched on the torch at 1700 and the Russians said, enough, let's get out of here. So we crawled through the lightening holes, getting thoroughly wet in the process, and I cut my thigh which with rust and dirt in it took a long time to heal. We gathered by the manhole cover, and Alex removed the iron bars from the handles and tried to push the plate out over the studs but it would not budge. We realised the pirates had got through to the other side, put the nuts on the studs, and wound them up. We were bolted into the tank. Our sanctuary had become our prison, and potentially our tomb.

Ted Burke of course, was on the outside, either still hidden or in the hands of the pirates. Either way we hoped he would be working towards our release. At intervals we gave three thuds on the steelwork with an iron bar to indicate we were ready to parley. In theory we could have been left in the tank all night with only water, and the air getting fouler by the hour. I felt a clammy sweat. I also feared one of the Russians might get a panic attack and start screaming or fighting, but they kept cool. I thought what an inconvenient time and place to have a heart attack or stroke, but banished those negative feelings. I reassured the Russians that we were worth more alive than dead, and just counselled patience. But it weighed heavily on my conscience that I had got us all into this mess which in the circumstances was appalling. From hero to villain, just like that.
We had entered the tank about 0100 and at 1900 we heard the sound of a spanner working on the nuts, and nuts falling and trickling away. Then Somali voices and a sudden shaft of

light as the manhole cover was pulled away. A great lifting of spirits tinged with anxiety that we might be punished for the trouble we had caused.

"Captain Colin come hout! Captain Colin come hout!" I hastened to obey but a tremendous bang and smoke sent me reeling back against Berezovskiy. We thought we had been shot but the shouting continued so we clawed our way through the smoke and out through the manhole to face the wrath of Omar. Alexander was pushed and shoved towards the engine room to start the generators, and the rest of us were bundled up through the escape hatch onto the aft deck to be surrounded by shouting leaping pirates firing their guns in the air. Whirling dervishes' came to mind. Were they happy or were they mad? It was hard to tell. But then Ahmed sidled up to me and whispered,
"Don' worry Captain, nobody shot, nobody shot, I (in) charge!" That was very reassuring and we let them have their fun, celebrating our recapture. We were tripped and pushed to the deck, soon joined by Alex who had started a genny and restored lights to the ship. "Where's Ted, where's Ted?" They demanded. I replied that I had no idea, he had not been in the tank with us, so a search began. Ted later said that in his deep narrow hiding place he had heard the searchers, and thin shafts of torch light had penetrated between the slats of a grating over him, but they found him not. He emerged finally when he considered it wise and safe to do so.
But now Omar gestured for us to rise and follow him to the bridge, where he ordered the Russians to lie on the deck, to starboard of the consul. Lastly he confronted me as I stood there dripping and looking contrite. He snorted, shook his head slowly, eyes fixed on mine, and said,
"Captain Colin. Captain Colin." Then he grinned and held out his hand, which I shook dumbly, then pointing to the port side of the consul he said,
"Sil-leep!"and with a few words to the assembled gunmen he swept out. Well, I thought, that wasn't too bad. Rather like losing a good game of squash, respect on both sides. I was dreadfully weary but shivering and teeth chattering prevented sleep until a heavy blanket landed on me and I just caught sight of the man who had thrown it. It was Omar. Not such a bad swine after all. Ted appeared next and lay down in the centre, between port and starboard consuls, and this was to be our sleeping pattern for the next thirty five days. The warship was still there, cruising up and down, useless bastards, just a paper tiger, as the Chinese say, no teeth or claws.

13th February, Wednesday.

All six of us were kept in the wheelhouse day and night. Someone brought my mattress which fitted beside the consul, kinked up against the window forward and the Aldis signal box aft, but comfortable enough. On the starboard side the four Russians were much more cramped, with one mattress and a few blankets and pillows between them. Ted had the centre alley to himself but whenever the pirates wanted to use the VHF or SSB radios they had to avoid stepping on him, or he moved.

 Komkov was allowed to go to the galley to fix the gulag soup, under armed guard, and Ted or Alex occasionally checked the engine room, with a gunman. The boatdeck chest freezer was found to be defective so contents transferred to the other one below. On a toilet visit I saw how my locked toilet door had been viciously assaulted. The steel hinges had been struck heavily with an edge tool, perhaps a fire axe. The door handle bent downwards. The door itself, a thick fire door was deeply gouged. And the door frame, a box section alloy construction had a hole right through it at about waist height, through which my middle finger could pass. I assumed this to be a bullet hole but lining up the holes in the box section I could see no corresponding mark on the shower bulkhead. Sometime later I was told this hole was driven through in order to see if I was inside. As I made no sound they feared I had hanged myself.

I also discovered that before they broke into the thrusters compartment and saw the aft peak manhole had been opened they suspected we had all jumped overboard and swum ashore. So three or four, including the schoolmaster swam to the beach and searched for us among the bushes. Several times we were asked why we had done what we did. They reasoned that we had food and water, as much freedom of movement as could be expected, and generally were well cared for. They evidently did not imagine that we were expecting an attack from the warship which would result in some or all of them being dead. The only explanation I offered was that it was a prisoner's duty to try to escape. We also emphasized that we had failed miserably and now accepted that we were prisoners and would not misbehave again. For my part this was genuine, and I set about regaining the trust which I had forfeited. When I requested a toilet visit, or a slightly longer trip to wash and shave, or fetch water from the wheelie bins to flush the toilet, I did exactly that, without any attempted diversions, intending to be a model prisoner.

Ted, on the other hand, said this was just a setback, and he would continue to scheme. He described at length some American film hero who had frequently escaped and been caught, been beaten and thrown in a hole, but each time, playing with a baseball, had planned his next manoeuvre. I believe the pirates sensed this in Ted and never trusted him. He was always testing the limits. On a "toilet" trip he would be gone for ages, and reported that he had dhobied some clothes, checked fridges and foodstore, and pinched a few cashew nuts for us. I somewhat despaired of him, and distanced myself from him, so that we were not thought to be scheming together. I also realised that Ted's way of dealing with the stress was different from mine. He needed to be active, whereas I was now content to play the waiting game. We had given the owners and Americans a chance to be proactive and they had failed us. Furthermore my role was to be an impartial mediator between the pirates and David Green, the owner's spokesman. Lastly I knew that my hasty acquiescence in the failed plan had endangered the Russians as much as us, and I owed it to them not to undertake any more rash actions.

14th February, Thursday.

All day and night spent in the wheelhouse. In the 1400 phone call to David Green he explained that the Danish government, in line with other western governments, was taking steps to prevent the international movement of large sums of money to pay criminals. I passed this on to the pirates who were not impressed. The sum accumulated in Dubai remained the same. Today we heard that two people had been killed ashore and four injured. By warship's guns or government troops we could not tell.

15th February, Friday.

Last night Ted somehow managed to spend several hours in the messroom discussing the ransom with the one we called Anthony Quinn, whose real name ended with Farrar or Farrah. He was certainly one of the senior pirates and spoke quite good English. He had three wives and a lot of children. He had worked in Dubai as a chauffeur, but the job ended when he fell asleep at the wheel causing an accident which had killed an Arab. Farrah was thrown into gaol for twenty one days, stripped of his licence and visa and deported.

This was how Ted described the lengthy discussion. After talking about families and football they got around to the ransom. Ted said they would never get the US$2.5 million demanded and should start with a more realistic figure like $1.5 million. Farrah explained that realistically they had incurred expenses which, apart from anything else must be recovered. So Ted took a sheet of paper and made a list, commencing with the $427,000 already on the table. There were the two boats lost in the initial attack, X amount of dollars, plus the three outboard engines, and some ammunition. Then there was the cost of maintaining the camp ashore, wages, loss of earnings, food for us, cigarettes for the Russians, weed for the pirates, petrol for running the boats. The list went on and on, and when finally tallied up came to US$900,000. (A considerable improvement on 2.5 million.)

In the morning Ted could hardly wait to tell me of this breakthrough, and when I learned that the pirates on board, and some "manager" ashore had also agreed to this figure, I too felt enthusiastic and relieved. The narrowing of the gap was surely great news, and I got permission to inform the Copenhagen owners by email, copied to our Dutch office. I allowed Ted to sign it off, which he did with a flourish, "Gentlemen I can do no more!"

This was the day the warship asked that all six hostages should speak to them in turn to convince them that we were all still alive, as they normally only heard my voice. Omar reluctantly agreed. All performed in turn giving their name, rank, and some assurance that they were in good health, except Ted who had to remark on various afflictions, bad back etcetera. The last one to grasp the VHF handset, very gingerly, was Kimochkin, who stood there dumbly looking at me. I told him,
"Just say your name, and OK." So he said, "Name, OK" and dropped the phone. Pirates and crew laughed and Berezovskiy coaxed him into trying again,
"Pyotr Kimochkin, OK."

I reflected ruefully that on an ISM form I had ticked the box saying I had handed him his personal safety instruction manual, written in English, and that he had read and understood it. I asked the warship to stand off a couple of miles at this sensitive time, which they did. All slept in the wheelhouse again that night.

Before moving on I would like to dwell on the importance of the breakthrough which Ted achieved in reducing the ransom demand and which has never been acknowledged.

It received no publicity because after our release we were all exhorted not to disclose details of the ransom. But at the time it had great significance. I believe the owners would have been happy to pay the US$900,000 to get their ship and crew back. After our release the sum actually paid appeared widely in the press, beginning I believe with a report from East Africa. The usual form was, "Crew released after ransom of US$700,000 paid." The implication being that the sum demanded and paid was the same. My notes show that on the day the $900,000 figure was agreed upon as a realistic starting point, tension reduced on board. Pirates and crew felt that progress was being made. I don't think Ted ever received a word of thanks for his important contribution.

16th February, 2008.

Although my notes did not record the day Omar Said, or Saheed, or Sayeed, came aboard I think it was this day. He deserves a description. We called him Omar 2.

He was dressed differently, dapper in matching khaki slacks, shirt, and pork pie hat. The pirates deferred to him and referred to him laughingly as "royalty." He never held a gun, and said he was not a pirate. In the course of several conversations, for his English was good though halting, he told me his family had fled Somalia when the government collapsed in 1991. He was aged twelve then which made him twenty nine in 2008. Asked if he was a government official he laughed and said,
"No, I was sacked." Asked if he was descended from royalty he again laughed but replied, "Sort of." I then enquired when Somalia last had a king, and he promptly replied, 1920. He went on,
"I am here to see that you are being properly cared for." At whose behest? I wondered.

Since being home I have checked Somali history and seen that in 1920 the Somali guerrilla leader Mohammad Bin Abdullah, the "mad mullah" was killed by a chance bomb. Was he Omar's ancestor?

I have also seen this report on the internet:-
SOMALIA; A local media outlet alleged confidential sources reported that a government official had been detained on allegations of having links with the pirates (Svitzer Korsakov) per 24 Feb 08 reporting. According to the article, Omar Shafdero employee at the Puntland Ministry of Finance, was arrested on 05 Feb 08 on the order of Puntland President General Mohamud Adde Muse. The article cites sources close to the president as explaining that President Muse accused Shafdero of being closely associated with the group of pirates holding the highjacked tug. Shafdero was reported quickly released under mysterious circumstances with a source in Bosaaso suggesting corruption at all levels contributed to the release. Was this our Omar 2?

Whatever the background of Omar 2 he had a benign effect on board the tug. He got the pirates to thoroughly clean my bathroom and Ted's and saw that we had keys to keep them locked for our exclusive use. He also had the messroom cleaned, even joining in himself, as it had become filthy with the scattered remains of the Qat. Henceforth the messroom was kept locked except at our mealtimes. When on board Omar 2 slept in there on a settee. One day he remarked that the Russians all smoked heavily but Ted and I did not. I agreed, and commented that we liked a drink but our beer and wine had all been looted. Omar promised to do something about that. He generally stayed on board a few days and then disappeared for a similar period ashore. It was said he had an expensive four wheel drive vehicle at the top of the cliff. On his next return he produced a bottle of BALEZAF gin distilled and bottled in ADDIS ABABA, which he kindly gave to me after taking a hefty swig or two himself. It was very welcome. Over the course of the next few weeks I believe he delivered in total three of these bottles of gin, though one never knew how much the bottle would contain after he had sampled it.

Omar Saheed also told me a strange tale about his birth. He was one of identical twin boys, but born forty eight minutes apart. It seems the woman assisting believed there was only one and cleaned up and left, so that the second boy arrived unaided. The twin brother is in Dublin, and still looks exactly like Omar apart from having hair, while Omar is shaved completely bald, closely resembling Yul Brynner in "The King & I."

I imagined that this Omar avoided touching guns and being too closely associated with the pirates, in anticipation of some future role in the government of the country. They need people like him, educated and humane, and with a sense of humour. On one occasion he carried a goatherd's crook stick, which I admired and handled. He said,
"You like it? You have it," and insisted that I did. I have it with me here now.

17th February, Sunday.

Spent most of the day and all night in the wheelhouse. Omar Hassan and the teacher ashore.

When Omar was ashore he left command either to Farrah or a veteran we nicknamed "Steptoe". He had streaks of grey in his goatee beard and cared nothing for his appearance, wearing dark robes and rags thrown on in a casual way. He showed a missing tooth in the lower jaw when he smiled, and generally I got along well with him. He seldom got excited. One day I saw him practicing with the machine gun. He sat on the boat deck, legs either side of the gun on a tripod, with the ammunition belt lying on the deck. Another pirate stood pouring oil onto the gun from one of our engine room cans. Steptoe's bursts of fire homed in on a fisherman's buoy several hundred yards away and had the buoy dancing in the spray the shots were throwing up. I was impressed and told him so, which earned a toothy grin.

On one of these days during my routine 1400 call to David Green I asked if these calls were recorded, and received the blunt reply, "No." Ted and I could not believe it. How remiss of them; we were dismayed at this news. Not surprising they had not understood my barely coded message to the warship to watch for our blackout and then attack.

In the debriefing which followed our release we were assured that all talks had indeed been recorded, replayed, and analysed. So they must have got the message. Did they choose not to act upon it, not to relay it to the warship? Or did the warship receive the message but decide not to act?

18th February, Monday.

Quite a relaxed atmosphere in the morning which raised our hopes, and an Arabic, or Somali message came in for the militia.
In the 1400 call David Green denied receiving Friday's message about the $900,000. He merely asked how long our fresh water would last.

Today I sent an email to the Dutch office telling them about plans to run the ship ashore, shoot the Russians, and take me and Ted into the desert for further ransom.

19th February.

At 0700 I was allowed to speak to the warship 064, USNS Carney. Ted had a brief chat about his back trouble but when asked what medication he was taking he was prevented from replying. Omar Hassan and the warship's Omar had a long talk and Hassan even laughed, which we took as an encouraging sign. An American officer had explained to me that their Omar had emigrated from Djibouti to the USA as a boy but retained his language, and upon joining the Navy had been assigned to interpreting for ships in Somali waters. The pirates accepted this cover story, confirmed to me that he had a Djibouti accent, and clearly did not regard him as a traitor working for America, though America was a despised nation.

All of us, two by two were allowed out of the wheelhouse to exercise in the sun. Ted and I took full advantage of this but the Russians didn't much care for exercise.
At 1400 David Green came up with a new figure of US$678,000 available, and convincing arguments re the Danish government asking questions and would stop the movement of

money if they found out. In support of this offer Green said a Danish tanker with twenty crew was ransomed last year for $550,000 so this offer was good.

Our pirates' comment was, "Another militia, not us."

I had goat and rice today. The rest of the crew generally spurned Somali food except chapattis, but I accepted it in order to play down cultural differences between us. I also noticed they gave me good cuts of lean meat, so rejection might have been hurtful.

Sammy Davis Junior was trussed up today on the afterdeck for two hours without any explanation to us. They took me along to see him. His ankles had been tied together and his wrists behind his back. Then the four joints had been drawn together so that he was bow shaped, belly to deck, writhing and whimpering. Ted and I were surprised as he normally kept out of trouble with Omar, and wondered if it was just a show for us, a bit of terror.

After a long meeting I was informed at 1745 that the $678,000 offer had been rejected.

20th February.

0600 toilet and shave. Good chicken and chips lunch, Ted and I chewing garlic cloves.

1400 phone call David Green simply repeated that there was no more money. Omar Hassan appeared to urge acceptance. I was hopeful and passed the word that when the deal was finally done I would join them in a chewing of QAT, which they greeted with glee. They frequently offered me the weed but I explained that I had never smoked or taken drugs, and didn't intend to start.

21st February, Friday.

A second warship on scene, so we were all confined to the wheelhouse under the guns, and extra gunmen came from ashore. More weed and dry gin came with the new personnel. When I phoned David Green he said the cash was already in Dubai. He suggested a hotel handover and would supply a contact name and number, and when the pirates' man phoned he would be given a password, so that when they met Green's man would know it was the right person. A phone call to the ship would then trigger our release. We finally got them to agree to the $678,000 figure and Omar Hassan, Farrah, and the mullah, Abdul Azziz went ashore to decide on the handover man. I think it safe to assume they went to debate this with superiors ashore as they sometimes referred to a "manager." The experts in our debriefing asserted that there was always a "Mister Big" behind the pirates who are merely foot soldiers. I'm not entirely convinced in this case as they were so amateurish, and fractious.

22nd February.

In the early hours of the morning a folded note fluttered down on me from Ted. When sure this had not been seen I carefully unfolded it and read:-
"Two sick Singapore seamen on board, repatriation, humanitarian gesture."

I was delighted. This meant various things and I could hardly wait for daylight to get more details. Meanwhile my imagination ran wild. I had heard that two of the crew of the highjacked Singapore fishing vessel off Eyl fourteen miles down the coast were ill. This could mean our pirates were anticipating our imminent release. I speculated that they might not be seriously ill, just feigning sickness to get free, and once at sea with us would soon recover. All Chinese can cook and I envisaged them taking over the galley and producing some terrific meals. At last daylight arrived and one by one we made our toilet calls accompanied of course by a gunman. As soon as possible I said to Ted,
 "Great news, but I heard no boat in the night, when did they come aboard?"
"Oh!" said Ted, "They are not here, I just thought it a good idea, what do you think?"

The pirates had left me a large section of goat vertebra the previous night, but I could not face it cold in the morning.

Strong N.E.monsoon today. Concerned for the anchor I paid out to six shackles.

Some of the pirates wanted to know just how the handover of cash would take place, so with the schoolteacher watching and translating every step of the way I took a sheet of paper and pen. In the middle of the page I drew a smart palladian entrance with steps, and potted palms either side, and labelled it "Hotel."
Then from the right hand bottom corner I "walked" my fingers up to the entrance, saying, "David Green's man Mustapha Camel." Immediately they asked who was he? Was he Somali? Patiently I explained it was just a name I had given him for the sake of illustration. Anyway, I continued, he goes to reception and explains that he is expecting a friend to meet him there, and meanwhile will take a coffee. I "walked" him across to the top right hand corner, all eyes following so as not to miss anything.
Sometime later, 12 o'clock or whatever time had been agreed, your man Ali Baba appears. An even louder outcry,

"Who is he? Is he Somali?" Again I explained it was just a name I had given him, appropriate as in history he led a gang of forty thieves. When this was translated they thought this a great joke, and the name Ali Baba was frequently on their lips. Well Ali Baba would go to reception and be directed towards Mustapha Camel at the coffee table. They craned their necks to follow this, excited like children. The two men would shake hands, drink coffee, and finally Ali Baba would walk out with the money. That is how I imagined it would happen.

They gabbled among themselves as they mulled it over, then put a question to me through the schoolteacher.
"When do they count the money?"
"Well for goodness sake how do I know? They must figure it out, I can't do it all, I'm here!"

1430 The pirates' business friends in Dubai would not risk their businesses, visas, reputations, or gaol to help. The pirates now wished the money to go to Djibouti, meaning further delay. I then questioned how Mustapha Camel was supposed to fly the bags of cash to Djibouti, get through airport procedures, and rendezvous with Ali Baba without being robbed, or having his luggage impounded. I asked Sancha how they had got the money from previous highjackings, and his rather lame reply was,
"He was a t'ief." Meaning the go between. This confirmed my opinion that this crowd were rank amateurs at piracy, still learning the trade.

23rd February, Saturday.

The US warship enquired how we were keeping and I declined to report all well as we were living like pigs, penned in the wheelhouse, getting dirtier by the day, with no facilities, comforts, or basic freedom. As this was translated Omar Hassan looked uncomfortable. So I asked if Komkov and Kimochkin could be allowed to use their cabins, as they had no hand in our attempted escape, yet were being punished equally. Also as he could appreciate those two would be quite incapable of planning or carrying out any "monkey business." If they were below in their cabins the rest of us would have more space to stretch out, especially at night. Omar agreed, and I felt I had gained an important concession, and thanked him with one of my rare uses of the Arab word, "shokran," (thank you.)

The pirates were arguing all day and I believe Omar must have gone ashore that night as my notes show him returning the next day.

24th February.

Ted Burke had an assortment of Australian, Irish, and United Kingdom documents, passports, and professional papers, and on this day reported them missing

At 1100 Omar Hassan returned aboard under fire from the warship. He brought bottled water, cigarettes and other useful things, plus Qat. Due to the firing we were all confined in the wheelhouse.

1400 David Green's man had transferred to Djibouti but I was told that getting the money there could take a week.

25th February, an eventful day.

Boats were shot at twice as they came and went with stores including a rare treat for us, lobster tails. The Americans deployed two fast ribs (rigid inflatable boats) and an airborne robot camera.

I fell out with Ted for leaving the water pump on for three hours allowing the pirates to shower, while we were living like pigs. Alexander Lichkunov put it this way,

"Pirate monkeys take shower, but fuck dirty Rooshians!" There would be no more water pumping. Water would henceforth be carried up from the engine room in five gallon containers to the galley for cooking and drinking. Sea water would be used for dish washing and toilet flushing.

Ted cooked the lobster tails for lunch which went some way to restoring harmony between him, me, and the Russians.

At 1400 David Green said after the ransom was paid and we were released a new crew could relieve us at Colombo, but we all expressed the desire to complete the voyage to Singapore as per contract.

26th February, Tuesday.

Loose toilet for me at 0400 and 0600, but not as bad as Ted yesterday.
All crew obliged to speak in turn to the warship to reassure them we were all alive.

Today the militia came up with a new initiative. They described four or five Somali money transfer facilities, something like banks with branches in many countries, used by overseas

Somali workers to transfer money home. One was called Amal, and another Dahabshiel. The sum transferable daily was limited, but if Mustapha Camel and Ali Baba went together to each facility the whole ransom could be transferred to Bosaaso within a week.

At 1400 I phoned David Green with this new idea which he said his team would consider. In the ensuing euphoria I was given a bottle of Addis Ababa gin and drank some of it with Omar Hassan, Omar Saheed, Gele, and a couple of loafers. In conversation I learned that Omar had been a paratrooper in the legitimate army when Somalia had a government. Pointing to a 10 kopek coin on the deck I explained that it had been there when we left St.Petersburg and I had left it there for "luck," but it had not brought me much luck so far. Hassan picked it up, decided the Peter The Great side was for bad luck, and spun it twice. He was highly amused to see "bad luck" both times.

27th February.

At 0600 I helped Ted and two pirates carry containers of water up from engine room to galley. The fresh water situation getting more serious; for cooking and drinking only, no dhobying of clothes. I occasionally soaped and rinsed the armpits of shirts, with about a litre that had first served to clean my teeth, wash and shave, and finally it flushed the toilet. The Somalis clean their teeth with a mswaki twig which bushes out making an efficient brush.

The warship anchored for the first time, on our starboard bow, and launched two ribs which stationed themselves on our starboard quarter, but nothing interrupted the passage to and fro of our supply boats over the shallow space between us and the beach.

1400 Told David Green that tomorrow we should be able to provide a contact name and number in Dubai. Also reported our satcom. paper running out, with no spare rolls. This paper had been mainly used up printing endless warnings of the pirate threat off Somalia, and America's intention to stamp it out. This kind of communication being "urgent safety" cannot be blocked out, but it grieved me to watch our precious paper churning out onto the deck with all that repeated blurb.

28th February, Thursday

0200 to toilet. Stools like milky coffee. At 0600 I found I had leaked right through my sarong into the mattress. To toilet, cleaned up and put on fresh pants, shorts, and shirt.

Turned the mattress over, and after breakfast rinsed out the sarong.

Last night the navy officer on duty had been "Juliette" and I let Berezovskiy handle the call. I heard her ask what requirements we would have when we finally left this place. She said diesel, water, and food could be supplied in quantity.

Witnessed Anthony Quinn giving a thorough telling off to Fife and others and I was amused to hear him resort to the English word "emergency."

At 0800 Gele the interpreter returned with reports that there had been a long argument between those in favour of money in Djibouti or Dubai. Perhaps when the two Omars returned we would learn who won.

At 0845 Berezovskiy came with a pirate complaining of a sore kidney, right side. Gave him some tablets and sympathy, and advised him not to sleep on cold steel decks. I suggested it might be his cold Kalashnikov pressing against the kidney and recommended a change of job, perhaps a return to goatherding.

The December 6th 2007 Daily Telegraph newspaper I distributed on the bridge was very popular with Ted and the two Russians who could read it. Ted took copious notes from the shares page, planning a big stock market killing when he got home. He had been studying a textbook on "charting" and appeared totally won over by the arguments in favour of plotting graphs. He came out with all the jargon. Privately Nikolai and I agreed that if it was that certain and easy all chartists would be millionaires.

My honey pot drained and rinsed. Still eating a few raisins from hideaways.

1400 phone call. David Green said cash could be in Djibouti by Tuesday or possibly Monday, if the militia wished, but no senior pirates were here to decide.

1720 Told off the schoolteacher who flopped down on my settee with a grin. I told him I needed some "alone time." On the bridge and everywhere else there were people and sometimes one just needed time alone. So he buggered off nonplussed, and I finished the gin bottle.

At that point in the siege we felt that as we were completely compliant with their wishes or orders, and were doing our best to help them get their money, they should otherwise leave us alone. They, on the other hand, regarded us as their prisoners, completely at their mercy, and beck and call. They continued to open our cupboards and drawers, and ask questions, not so much out of interest as to practise their English. They annoyed us by fiddling with controls and switches on radars and radios, out of curiosity and boredom. Ted's constant writing of notes clearly irritated them. I wrote mine discreetly, when they were not looking. If they chose they could have picked them up and thrown them into the sea. Relations were mostly congenial, but they were volatile, especially under the influence of Qat and one had to be wary. Compared to Ted I kept myself at arm's length. They doubtless considered him more fun, more entertaining, and that suited me. He sometimes played dominoes with them.

29th February, (leap year), Friday.

The galley freezer was not working so the contents were transferred to the freezer in the store room.

A rare email arrived from my wife, hopeful of our early release. She had been talking to my original girlfriend which pleased me. Whatever happened to me I would have liked her to know. It was a kind gesture typical of Barbara.

At 0820 the two Omars returned and I was reassured that all would be resolved this day or the next. They had a business man in Dubai prepared to take the money in one lump sum and fly it straight out. When he was airborne we would be released. They gave me another bottle of gin after Omar 2 had done his usual quality control sampling.
At 1015 some anticipated men arrived, strangers to me, and went into conference.

At 1330 I phoned David Green and told him to hold the money in Dubai as they definitely wanted it there, though they could not agree on the man to receive it. A decision had been made to allow more time for argument. Finally they said the man's name and phone number would be given at 1400 on Sunday, and the money transferred and ship released Sunday afternoon. We would see.

I always shared good news with Ted and the Russians. Generally Ted accepted it unequivocally and pumped water in celebration, which worried me. The Russians were invariably sceptical, pessimistic, and the friction between them and Ted at times approached open hostility

On this leap year day I overheard Ted explaining to the Somalis how in our country women are permitted to propose marriage to men. I kept completely out of that discussion believing it would lead nowhere, and possibly to trouble. For macho Muslims with up to four wives, and a feudal divorce code, to be told of this bizarre Christian custom would only lead to them looking upon us with contempt. My policy was always to downplay the cultural differences between us, and portray ourselves as ordinary working men like them, struggling to make a living in a harsh world. When asked about my pay I avoided the question, and turned it to advantage by saying my pay would have been stopped when I lost the ship, and would only be resumed when the owners got their ship back. Therefore I was as keen as them to see a resolution of the impasse. During World War II British seamens' pay stopped when ships were sunk, though the men might spend days or weeks in lifeboats. Shipowners are known for hearts of stone, not gold.

After the evening gulag soup I managed to get Ted to join me in the cabin for a couple gins and a chat, despite much chuntering from Gele. But we slept in the wheelhouse as usual.

1st March 2008.

0600 Didn't quite make it to the toilet so filthy sarong and pants to wash.

That morning the pirates bought two fish from a fisherman and caught a few more so all hands had a fish dinner. Personal questions came from David Green which would be put to each of us before the ransom was handed over, to prove we were all alive. For example "What is the name of your dog?" "Who is your wife's best girlfriend?" "What was the number of your apartment when you were first married?" A couple of the Russians had problems with the questions, which had been provided by their wives.

This day the satcom. paper ran out. Henceforth any emails would have to be read off the screen and hastily written down, subject to the gunman's permission to approach close enough to see. He was always nervous about us standing too close to the muzzle of his Kalashnikov as he guarded the set against our unauthorized use.

2nd March, Sunday

Evgeny Komkov took over the cooking exclusively being marginally better than Kimochkin, though he was very surly and threatened to throw down his tools and walk out when Ted offered advice.

This day had started with high hopes but the Omars and other leaders arrived aboard late, having failed to persuade up to "fifty" Somali business men in Dubai to risk picking up the money. So we were deadlocked, no bank accounts, no passports, and no respectable friends.

At 1400 I told David Green to pay the satellite phone bill as we were under threat of being cut off. Apart from my brief daily calls the pirates used it all the time, and at $6 per minute it must have cost a fortune.

The warship returned on station having been absent for some time. We learned later these absences were to rendezvous with a refueler below the horizon.

3rd March.

There was a bit of a breakthrough this day. David Green reported that Amal bank was willing to transfer money to Somalia at possibly $50,000 per day. I gave Green a name for Garoowe, Mohammad Abdi Qaadir with a phone number. The pirates wanted $270,000 to go to him and the balance $408,000 to go to Bosaaso but they could not agree on a receiver there.

4th March.

I gave Green the required name and number for Bosaaso, but later he reported that the Amal bank and others would not help as they believed the two names were front men and not the genuine recipients. Also they required legal documents which could not be provided. All this incompetence and frustration led to harsh words between us and the militia, which I struggled to control. Calling them monkeys and eejits did not help. The bottled water almost finished and condensate severely rationed.

Some of the young hotheads were convinced David Green was playing a game which would result in them being attacked and deprived of their fortune. The answer was always to run the ship ashore and shoot the crew. Even Ted doubted the sincerity of the owners, convinced that with their resources they could find a way to deliver the cash if they really wanted to. I feared the pirates might shoot or mutilate one of us to instil a sense of urgency; "pour encourager les autres." Ted bore the main brunt of the threats, due I think to his chattering and scribbling of copious notes which they found irritating and suspicious. He also outspokenly called them fools, amateurs, and no hopers, which if translated must have grated on them. By this time we both detested the schoolteacher who hung around us, alternately cajoling, confiding, and trying to bully us.

5th March, Wednesday.

At last a significant breakthrough. David Green informed us that the money would be in Somalia on Sunday or Monday. His man, a Somali or Arab speaker would be in Garoowe on Friday or Saturday and required a phone number and name of contact there, to arrange a safe place to meet.

Our Dutch satcom now broke down. Something was wrong with the A drive and it would not connect with satellites. Nikolai worked on the ship's computer but could make no internet connection, ACCESS DENIED. He thought it possible the Russian fax machine would receive but not transmit.

The Somalis' flour and our flour said to be finished. All bottled water had been consumed and the mixture of good fresh water and air conditioning condensate in the main tank was strictly rationed. The pirates were very edgy and occasionally fired a few rounds into the sky or sea. I chewed cashew nuts and took special care not to do anything provocative.

When the warship requested a chance to photograph the hostages, to convince themselves we were all alive, it was a welcome relief from the tension and I had little trouble getting Omar's agreement. We lined up along the foreside of the bridge and I happened to see a puff of smoke on the warship followed by a dull thud as a small robot 'plane was projected into the sky. Equipped with a camera it was remotely controlled to fly around the tug about a hundred feet up, taking pictures. I noticed the schoolteacher and Farrah covered their heads but most of the pirates brazenly sat with guns in their laps watching the robot. One fellow tried to shoot it down but the robot flew on unperturbed, until it was retrieved by directing it into a net on the warship.

6th March.

The "tooth" barged into my bathroom as I was washing, cursed, and barged out. He was a nasty bit of work. As we had helped him relieve some severe toothache early on we had hoped for some goodwill in return, but never got it. One evening as he and Sancha and the gunman guarding the satcom were chewing Qat and quietly chatting I began teasing Sancha by saying he should not take too much weed, as he needed a clear head next day for the telephone. Sancha and the other chuckled but the "tooth" shot me an evil look and spat out some vile comment which instantly swept the smiles from the other faces, and left them silent for a long time. I turned away, wondering just what threat or curse he had uttered, and resolved to be extra wary in his presence. He seemed to be one of Omar Hassan's favourites, and Omar didn't have many friends.

There was a panic that evening. The tender with two pirates drifted away at dusk. I saw one of them wave an empty fuel can and shout, so the problem was clear. Gele explained it was a common occurrence as there were many boats lined up along the shore, used indiscriminately by fishermen and militia who rarely checked the fuel. Darkness descends rapidly in the tropics and soon the boat was out of sight and nobody ashore responded to the radio calls for help. Our rescue boat was hastily launched and two gunmen went off to search, eventually assisted by another boat from the beach, but they returned late in the evening with no success. The monsoon wind and current ran south west parallel to the coast and I calculated how many miles they would drift before daylight. Ted and I speculated that they might have a bucket or plank to paddle obliquely towards the breakers, but privately I didn't much care if they lived or died. It would be two less making a living from terrorising seamen.

7th March, Friday.

In the morning the two men were reported safe in Eyl.

This day David Green announced he had to go away for a week on business and one Paul Smith would take over his duties. The pirates didn't take kindly to Green disappearing like that. They accepted him as the "owner" and resented being passed on to a presumed underling. As usual I shrugged and said it was nothing to do with me and beyond my control. I did not associate myself closely with Svitzer, the Dutch being my employers.

Today the satcom came back into limited life and I got out emails to Holland and Copenhagen. One of the Somalis made a point of telling me there was no HIV/AIDS in Somalia as the men slept only with their wives, and there was no prostitution or homosexuality. I nodded appreciatively without any expectation of testing these assertions.

8th March, Saturday.

Somali tea and chapatti for breakfast.

At 0940 completely without reference to the Chief Engineer Lichkunov changed generators. The Chief went to the engine room without seeking permission and therefore at risk of being shot, to find out why, and the Russian gave him loud abusive words to the effect that he, Lichkunov, was the real Chief Engineer. When Ted reported this to me I considered it serious enough to make an Official Log entry, and with Berezovskiy as interpreter and witness, I made it quite clear to Lichkunov that until Singapore he was Second Engineer under Ted Burke as Chief.

This fracas was observed by Omar Hassan who appeared to follow what was going on and made no attempt to interrupt. The problem stemmed from having owner's men involved in a Dutch delivery. The Dutch should never have agreed to it.

In my diary I recorded this day a feeling that the end was near, for better or worse. The owners had to find a way to deliver the money before the impatience of the gunmen resulted in blood letting. Ted was talking darkly about getting Hassan's approval to publicise our situation through an International news agency, by means of an email to his son. The object would be to cause maximum embarrassment to the prestigious owners who with their wealth and influence were pretending they could not get us out of our predicament. Ted hinted he might stir things up with various unions, including an Australian marine engineers' union to which he had once belonged. In his Walter Mitty mode he assured me he could put in train actions leading to the tying up of all Svitzer tugs in Australia. Personally I clung to the view that the owners were genuinely interested in paying the ransom for the ship. Their contempt for our welfare had been made apparent over the issue of cooks. I had a file of emails interchanged on that subject, including the final one from the Owner's Far East manager, an Estonian whose name meant "oak" in that language. I would dearly like to see him deposed.

The food situation was getting worse. There was no more chicken or fish, apart from ungutted local fish in the freezer. Flour deliveries depended on the Somalis, and flour bags had Kenya, Yemen, or Ethiopia marked on them. In fact we never saw anything at all manufactured in Somalia. Everything coming from abroad had to be paid for including the Qat which came from Kenya, and the pirates had run out of that.

There were long angry meetings today among the pirates who felt they were being messed about, and Ted agreed.

He spent several hours overhauling an old German compressor on deck belonging to the local shellfish divers. He said their bag of spares were all badly worn and though he was doubtful of much success the work kept him occupied. Burke was still agitating about his lost cameras and laptop, which could have been ashore and sold by this time, or in a cache on board for eventual return to us. It depended who you listened to. Burke believed he had identified the pirate who had taken the laptop and nicknamed him "Mohammad Laptop." He was probably the most evil looking of the brotherhood, and I never saw him in friendly chat with anyone. He pulsed with menace which repelled all who came near. Ahmed once said, "That man, killer!"

This day Paul Smith reported that his Somali now declared Garoowe too dangerous to deliver the money. They would now consider a sea delivery from Dubai starting Monday or Tuesday, but it would be difficult finding anyone brave enough to approach Somalia. Smith said they were also considering Mombasa, but our pirates always insisted the militias south of Eyl were more truly terrorists with political motives. I told Smith if we did rendezvous with a ship we would need water, food for fifteen days, and a cook. I gutted five good fish this evening with medical scissors for lack of a knife.

9th March 2008, Sunday.

With Omar Hassan's approval and without any interference or censorship from schoolmaster Gele I sent the following message to Svitzer copied to Holland:-

For 38 days our lives have had a money value. Without the prospect of money in exchange our lives and the ship have no value to the pirates
On 12th February we partly escaped for 19 hours. Since then we have been more closely confined.
The cost of keeping us increases daily with nothing produced locally, all bought from abroad with dollars. The moderates are losing control. Tragedy looms. No more words or delays
You should send a ship with the cash, a Somali speaker, an armed guard for self protection inward to Ras Asceyr.
We will meet you there, tracked by warship. Money transferred by unarmed tender with us still hostage.
Pirates depart for shore.

We, with other ship and warship proceed out of pirate range, then receive 10 tons water, a cook and food for 7 men 15 days. 2 case beer for Dutch employees, cigarettes for Svitzer.
F.O.Rob 107 MT (fuel oil remaining on board.)
This message uncensored and with approval of six crew; well but worried. Rgds Colin.

I thought that was dead clear and workable if they had the will.

For the first time I had told them how we had partly escaped for 19 hours on 12th February. If we should die I wanted that on record, we did not go like sheep into the ovens.

10th March 2008, Monday.

The day opened with a formal written complaint from the Chief Engineer about the dirty unhygienic state of the galley, "likely to foster gastro-enteritis and cholera."

I determined to refer the matter to the Chief pirate, and have it cleaned up.

The problem was threefold. We were very short of water and orders to clean the galley might result in a great sloshing around of the precious stuff and counter orders to stop! Secondly our two seamen who shared responsibility for our cooking had never had any training or experience in the job. They appeared to be peasants with no idea of food hygiene, bacteria, or anything else relevant to food handling. Thirdly the galley was shared with the pirates, several of whom took a hand in their cooking, also with no apparent comprehension of the health issues involved.

The 1400 phone call to Paul Smith was quite positive. They had got my email, and liked the idea of a sea transfer of the cash and my outline plan. They were working on it but told me emphatically not to move north. I was constrained in this call by several militia listening in, while Omar Hassan had asked me to keep it secret, which I also desired. So we were to stay where we were until further orders.

Smith also seemed keen for me to talk to the American warship, and on a channel other than 16. Whatever channel I spoke on the pirates would closely monitor the conversation and grab the phone and stop me if they did not approve.

Around 1700 there began repeated noises throughout the ship, very like a whistling kettle rising to the boil, receding, and rising rapidly again. We heard it on the bridge, in the engine room, and within the accommodation. One could not live with it. Omar Hassan immediately blamed Ted, "the usual suspect," and frog marched him down the engine room to stop the "alarms." Ted was able to show everything functioning normally, with no flashing red lights or other alarm indicators. So they came back to the bridge, and, faute de mieux, we concluded it must be the Americans. As the noise was becoming unbearable I obtained Omar's assent to call them. The Americans confirmed they were generating the noise harassment because we had not answered their calls for three days, and they required dialogue to ascertain that we were still alive. They stopped the noise on the understanding that we would henceforth have daily contact. Omar readily agreed. I have since learned subjection to the noise indefinitely results in vomiting, loss of balance, collapse, and death. How do they know, have they tried it on animals?

Meanwhile Hassan had ordered the starting of the main engines. Ted rose to comply but bad tempered Lichkunov had to be ordered to help. I then gave Berezovskiy a warning that if this attitude of Lichkunov continued I would put into Colombo and make crew changes. I knew Berezovskiy dearly wanted to complete the trip to Singapore and take over command, so it was up to him to keep the Second Engineer under control, or all four Russians would find themselves on the beach in Shri Lanka.

A new development enlivened the evening. A mysterious phone call came for the pirates from someone whom Ahmed and one we called "the Garoowe man" had contacted some days previously in Garoowe. He was said to be a Somali "ambassador" in Djibouti, and together with British, Irish, and Russian Embassies he was working towards our release. I was asked to spell out the names and nationalities of all the hostages, which as the connection was bad took a long time phonetically,
Komkov …. kilo oscar mike kilo oscar victor, and so on. I left the longest name, Nikolai Berezovskiy to last and by the time I got to it I was fed up with the exercise, and the guy at the other end was probably asleep. I failed to see how Embassies could achieve our release without paying ransom, which as tools of governments they were unlikely to do. However Ahmed and the other assured me the Spanish and Argentine Ambassadors had bought the freedom of two female journalists from those countries, so perhaps there was room for hope. Anyway this exercise entertained us all evening and I was told the result of the Ambassadorial conclave would be made known to us tomorrow at 1100 or 1200.

11th March, Tuesday

An email came in from Paul Smith which Nikolai read off the screen and said was mainly personal for Ted, but he was not allowed to see it until Gele returned from ashore to make sure the message was "innocent."

Cleaning of the galley commenced with instruction to use lots of disinfectant and no water.

At 0930 I had a visit from Omar Hassan and Ahmed who told me that they were the only two in whom I should confide regarding the delivery of the money. They advised me that if Paul Smith was determined to send the cash from the south I should warn him to keep 150 to 200 miles off the coast, especially a named place where the militia were linked to Al Queda and had a 75 horse power motor. They had repeatedly told me the pirates south of us were much more dangerous, motivated by politics and religion.

Hassan went ashore before midday and I snatched a quick talk with the warship. They asked me my destination once we were free, and I told them Singapore via Minikoi which they had never heard of, so I had to explain it was in the eight degree channel through the Maldives. Any merchant seaman would have known that.

The 1400 talk with Smith was very short. He said the money was "on the way" but would give no further details. Ted had so far waited seven hours to read the email from his wife but couldn't view it until Gele appeared to read it first, for hidden messages!

Omar Hassan returned in the evening but without the schoolteacher, so Ted's message still unread. Hassan had an ugly swelling below the right knee cap which Berezovskiy and I treated in my cabin, expressing a little pus and applying Russian antibiotics.

Omar Saheed gave me a bottle of gin half full, and all the pirates enjoyed a fresh supply of Qat, chewing diligently, and scattering stalks untidily. That night as we lay dozing fitfully on our mattresses the four gunmen on guard duty starting to sing, quietly and melodiously, as they passed around the weed. One sang the verses which I imagined to be a love story or some legend from their history, while the others softly crooned a tune which gently rose and fell, like the sands of a desert undulating interminably into hazy distance. There were many verses and the effect in that darkened wheelhouse, with stars arcing above us as the tug lazily rolled, was mystical, and I confess to a few silent tears.

12th March.

Omar Hassan came to my cabin for further treatment to his knee, and while he, Gele, Ted, and a couple of pirates were gathered together I thought it a good time to expound on my knowledge of Islam. I related how as a young officer I had worked for several months on a pilgrim ship carrying hadjis back and forth between Malaya and Jiddah. There had been a Koran on board in English, which I had read and learned how Jesus was regarded as an important prophet. I said I agreed with this view that he was a good and wise man, but no more divine than any other human. His name when alive was Iesu bin Yussuf, it was the Christians and particularly the Roman Catholics who later referred to him as Jesus son of Mary, implying that Joseph, though the father of James and a couple other brothers, was not the father of Iesu. At this Ted got up and walked out, but I felt I had gained some kudos with the Muslim pirates.

Ted's relationship with both Nikolai and Alexander was at a low ebb, and although tension would ease after our release I believed too much damage had been done. I therefore considered Colombo as the best, earliest option, to call and change crew, especially if Svitzer did not send a cook. Then I noticed the ship's register had expired on 29th February, which was alright as long as we were "on passage," even up to Singapore where the ship was to be reregistered under the Russian flag. But a call at Colombo would be inconvenient and expensive, and therefore unpopular with the owners.

At 1400 Paul Smith was non committal but said when the cash vessel was near we would be asked personal questions to prove we were alive, and then details of the ship and her arrival time would be revealed to us.

Gele the schoolteacher told me they were worried about being robbed by their friends ashore, and the whole operation of landing people, guns, and loot, would involve about four boat trips. Meanwhile he asked me to prepare notes for a lecture to his students who had been sadly neglected for weeks. The suggested subject was advice to boys on choosing a wife. Having been married three times, though consecutively not concurrently like a Muslim, I declared myself an expert and rattled off about a dozen paragraphs, starting with "beauty is only skin deep." I also stressed the importance of cooking, saying that in marriage you might have sex three times a week but you eat three times a day. Gele read it through slowly, questioning the odd word, and then solemnly declared that he would tell his students these were the wise words of an old English sea captain.

13th March, Thursday.

Around 0200 a female officer of the US warship called persistently. So with reluctant agreement of the armed guard I replied, partly to circumvent them putting the awful whistling noise through our speakers.

At 0900 warship 79 advised me that after release we were to proceed to Salalah in Oman, but I had no desire to go that way, circumnavigating Socotra and adding at least two days to the voyage.

At 1400 Paul Smith shocked us all by saying that the cash boat, at sea already three days in rough weather and following a circuitous route, would not reach us until Tuesday. Was it a bloody rowboat?

I prepared the following message to our Dutch boss but was not permitted to send it.

On departure should have fuel to reach Singapore at economy speed. More speed would require bunkers from supply ship or navy. Alternatively call at Colombo where Ted and I would leave as Anglo-Russian relations at a low ebb compounded by three months without a cook. Registry expired 29th Feb and our certificate endorsements 3rd March, which has to be considered. Please advise. Master.

14th March, Friday.

A beautiful morning with very light north easterly and almost no swell. The pirate cook brought my breakfast to the bridge. Somali tea, chapattis, and goat meat, lean and spicy.
Omar Hassan ashore so had a long chat with warship 79. I told them Ted was making copious notes to sell to Time magazine and have his face on the cover. Gele talked for an hour to the warship's Djibouti man. We later learned there was only one Djibouti man who rotated between the warships as they took turns to keep us company.

Omar Saheed half drunk by noon and when Hassan and Farrah came on board there was an immediate row resulting in Ahmed being bundled off the bridge and possibly tied up on the aft deck. I sometimes heard him referred to as Adani but he explained it was not his name. As a child he had been whiter skinned than most and had acquired the sobriquet Adani meaning white or pale, and those who had grown up with him still used it. This gang of pirates were inter related or of the same clan.

At 1400 Paul Smith confirmed the cash boat's ETA as Tuesday but would give me no other information. He asked if the militia would prefer any other location for the handover but I said this spot was optimal, in a safe anchorage and with the warship in attendance. To ask the pirates their preference would result in lengthy disputation so I didn't consult them.

Why couldn't Smith tell me anything at all about the personnel on the approaching vessel? Did she have a cook or Somali speaker? Was it a submarine or what? Did he not know? Was it all a trick? The Yanks had asked me to give the name of some Royal Navy coordinator in Bahrein to Svitzer, but why could they not tell them themselves? Were they not in touch with the owners, and if not why not? We were so much kept in the dark all the time, and the pirates baying for information and highly suspicious.

At 1600 Omar Hassan came for more attention to his knee and finally himself probed and removed a lump of gristle possibly enclosing shrapnel. We staunched the blood, filled the hole with antibiotic cream and lashed it up tight. Taking advantage of his gratitude I asked if Ted, who had bad diarrhoea, could sleep in his cabin close to the toilet. Omar reluctantly agreed but locked the cabin door and checked my bag of keys to ensure there was no spare. Berezovskiy, Lichkunov and I slept in the wheelhouse as usual.

March 15th Saturday.

I couldn't believe Ted's stupidity! With his own spare key he let himself out at around 0500 and went wandering. The guards went ape-shit and nearly shot him. Such a hard won privilege and he blew it. I told him off and upset him. He returned to bed and stayed there missing breakfast and didn't stir when the fire bells rang. The cause of that was tracked down to a glass fire alarm on the bridge broken by the "tooth" turning round and hitting it with his Kalashnikov.

No warship in sight. Had he gone off to meet the ship with our release papers, all six hundred and seventy eight thousand of them? The pirate captain's knee looked better but he would not keep the bandage on.

At 1400 Paul Smith confirmed the cash boat was on schedule for Tuesday but the crew was nervous about approaching the pirates' lair. I tried to reassure him that we had built a measure of trust between the pirates and us, and I was confident the handover could be accomplished calmly and safely. Hassan now confided in me secretly that he would not land the money here at Gabbac, which was too dangerous, but further up the coast at a place called Beyla, forty miles north. It was in fact one hundred miles.

Ted was required to sleep in the wheelhouse as expected following his foolish break out of the morning.

16th March, Sunday.

Dhobied two shirts and pants before breakfast.

There was goodwill in the air and I got permission for Nikolai to phone his wife in Sakhalin. She confirmed that our freedom was expected to happen on Tuesday.

Omar Hassan promised, as "service" to escort us ninety miles offshore once they had the money, to protect us from further pirate attack.

At 1400 Paul Smith announced the ship would arrive tomorrow morning, Monday, a day early. The crew were nervous and they had no Somali speaker. When free we were to proceed to Salalah in Oman where any crew wishing to leave would be able to do so.

Assisted by the schoolteacher I had a serious talk with Omar and persuaded him that I, rather than him, should dictate the logistics of the actual hand over. I claimed this right as I would be speaking to the deliverers in English, I had done most to get the money here, and he could trust me to complete the transfer into his hands. The delivery people would be nervous about coming close, fearing that they too could be highjacked, and we should send just a couple of unarmed pirates to collect. This was agreed.

At 1600 the crew had to answer personal questions to prove they were all alive. Alexander Lichkunov didn't know the name of his wife's best girlfriend and in a panic had to phone Russia to find out.

There was, as yet, no sign of the return of personal valuables said to be held in a cache, and Ted was still fussing about his laptop.

17th March, Monday. My daughter's birthday.

At 0200 Paul Smith phoned with the name of the delivery vessel and I was to call the Master "Martin." At around 0500 I made VHF and radar contact.

Martin was reluctant to approach too close to the coast with the pirates' encampment close behind us so I up anchored and moved further off shore. Omar wanted him to actually come alongside us but Martin had no intention of putting himself right under the guns of our total force, and he hovered about a half mile from us. Now came panic and confusion. The people ashore sensed something interesting was happening and came off in several boats waving AK47s and circling the delivery vessel like Red Indians round the wagons. So naturally the two boats we despatched were also heavily armed. Martin called for clarification as to which gunmen should be given the goods, but through binoculars I could not distinguish. Fortunately our lot managed to muscle their way in keeping the other wolves at bay, and in due course returned triumphant to us. As the job appeared to be done I managed a bit of a conversation with Martin. He complimented me on my handling of the whole highjacking from start to finish, which momentarily broke my composure. I personally felt it was him and his crew who deserved the praise. They had voluntarily come from a place of safety into a place of danger, which took courage, but without them delivering the ransom our situation would have been very serious. To the shipowner it was merely money but to us men bobbing about in little vessels at the mercy of crazy armed pirates high on Qat it was a matter of life or death.

Then suddenly a pirate rushed into the wheelhouse shouting that the money was not among the milk water biscuits chocolate etcetera they had. Martin said the schoolteacher had taken it and stowed it in a bow locker, but Gele shouted,

"Not me! I am here!" I realised that Omar Saheed's smart clothes had led Martin to think he was the teacher, and sure enough, Saheed had the cash, plus two bottles of scotch whisky which Martin had thoughtfully provided. I took charge of that after Saheed had helped himself, and the dollars went into the messroom under armed guard. I then released the delivery boat to return to Kenya, and suddenly feeling very lonely, assessed the situation.

Ahmed appeared wreathed in smiles,

"Captain you are free! You are free!"

Well I didn't feel very free. The pirates had the cash, the ship, and the hostages, all the cards. Could they be trusted? Could there be a sting in the tail from the "tooth" or Mohammad Laptop, the killer? Could Ted's insults come home to roost?

I returned the tug to precisely the same anchorage as before, and the pirates began counting and dividing the money in the messroom, Farrah superintending with a calculator. We crew were left alone so made various phone calls; to Holland who told me the whole crew would be relieved at Salalah; to my wife Barbara telling her the long nightmare was over, and to pass birthday greetings to my daughter.

At 1455 our rescue boat had to be launched to recover the pirates' boat which had slipped its mooring.

At 1500 the "tooth" walked into my cabin, opened the second drawer down and took the plastic key bag to conceal his share of the loot. I could not be bothered to object.

At 1600 I went to the bridge and found about fifteen of them all talking at once clustered around the "mullah" Abdul Azziz, with a calculator. Bedlam!

At 1615 Omar Saheed came to the cabin to top up his mug of scotch and explain that the debate above was going well, and showed me he had the key to the money. I refused him any more whisky saying that I had had a long day and my work was not yet over. I didn't want him getting drunk before the cash distribution was complete.

At 1635 Omar Hassan came to the cabin, gun slung as usual, and assured me most would go ashore that evening, leaving just seven to take north to Beyla. We shook hands on it.

At 1700 Ted awoke and I told him of the plans to relieve us at Salalah which should have pleased him, but he rushed up to the bridge to telephone Holland and complain about all the things he had lost, and demand compensation.

1900, not a soul disembarked. I had a blazing row with Ted about his f......g computer, an adult toy which he could replace, and surely would with Company dollars. The Somalis were struggling for the basic necessities of life, and he just kept on and on about cameras and laptop. One would have thought they had stolen his pacemaker.

Late in the evening most of the militia left the ship, and we set course for Beyla, with the remaining seven posted at vantage points on the look out for armed robbers, which gave rise to the bizarre Log entry, "Pirates on piracy watch."

18th March 2008.

Had my first shower for forty seven days. Two scrambled eggs, brown bread, and corned beef for breakfast, part of the goodies which came with the cash.

We arrived off the little village of Bandar Beyla around eight in the morning, and slowly circled while the pirates tried to contact the shore. Finally a passing fisherman agreed to take Anthony Quinn, Farrah, ashore to get help. He eventually returned with two of the usual white skiffs and at last the pirates disembarked, officially logged as 1018. There were no goodbyes. Omar Hassan had promised to escort us out to sea clear of other sea robbers, and one of the boats did stay with us for a few miles but then gave up and turned back.

We built up to maximum speed, about twelve and a half knots, and I made several phone calls announcing our freedom. An American warship reported that she was monitoring us from below the horizon! A fat lot of use that would have been if we were attacked again. We steamed due east for 100 miles and then turned north skirting Socotra Island and then a straight line to Salalah in Oman. After forty seven days it was fantastic to be free, but hard to get used to. I felt guilty lingering in my cabin.

19th March 2010

At 0300 a blazing row erupted between Burke and Berezovskiy, with Lichkunov adding fuel to the fire. Burke retired to his cabin and wrote me a long letter of explanation. Berezovskiy had angrily accused him of taking a black bag of his from the winchroom, which Burke had vehemently denied. Hot words led to fear of physical attack so Burke had locked himself in the cabin. He subsequently found he had indeed taken the wrong bag and apologised. The fact that such heat was generated over a trivial misunderstanding indicated how badly relationships had broken down. I did not bother to log the incident.

I had a talk with the Mate about Ted, pointing out his good points, and the difficulty we all had adjusting to a mixed crew of Dutch employed delivery men and owners' men, compounded by having no cook, and two seamen who spoke no English.

Berezovskiy's comment was that sometimes the Russians felt Burke was "like a child." I found that a curious assessment and pondered it at length. Mercurial and impulsive though he was, and certainly a Walter Mitty character with a history of grandiose schemes all ending in failure, yet dreaming still of great future success, he had run a good engine room. He had kept the machinery going, conserved fuel and water, and carried out all the statutory services, and maintained the engine log books.

Burke and I entered the after peak tank and retrieved iron bars, clothing, and bottled water which had been left there from our siege, and he pumped the tank dry.

In the evening well to the north east of Socotra we saw an approaching echo on the radar. It turned out to be USNS Carney, the main one keeping us company at the anchorage off Gabbac. They asked permission to pay us a visit, to which I agreed and they came in a fast inflatable. Three smart officers came to the bridge, a Lieutenant Commander, a Lieutenant, and a doctor. After introductions they warmly shook hands and said how delighted they were to meet us at the conclusion of our terrible ordeal. They all resembled the young President Kennedy, tanned, hair close cropped, and big smiles displaying such identically perfect white teeth, they appeared false.

After the effulgent greetings they placed a recorder on the chart table and fired questions. But I interrupted with a question of my own,
"Why did you not attack and rescue us when we blacked out the ship?" They shuffled, and answered slowly that though they had noticed the blackout they had received no warning message, and even if they had an attack to rescue four Russians, an Irishman, and an Englishman, putting US personnel at risk, would have required permission from above, way above, and they all rolled their eyes upward, and concluded that was unlikely to be granted. That dealt with, the interview proceeded in a more relaxed manner, and upon leaving they indicated they would like to bring us breakfast the following day.

20th March, Thursday.

Handing over the watch to Berezovskiy I went down one deck to watch preparations for receiving the American boarding party with breakfast. The two seamen had knocked out a few wedges and were battling with a big hammer to remove a large baulk of timber jamming the bulwark door shut. As they were attacking the wrong end I called to them to point out their folly, but they ignored me so I went down, grabbed the other end and easily disengaged it. I shouted at Komkov for being so stupid and obstinate and he yelled back at me in Russian and marched off for'ard.

The Americans duly arrived and boarded, two of last night's officers and cooks in cooks' hats carrying an enormous cool-box. These two chaps first thoroughly cleaned the galley, then started cooking, and spread a Carney crested tablecloth on the mess table. All kinds of shiny cutlery was deployed and plates with the ship's name and motto, "RESOLUTE,

COMMITTED, SUCCESSFUL." Ted bummed a plate as souvenir, and an officer instructed the cook to put that down as a breakage! Then came the breakfast, sausages, bacon, hamburgers, grits, eggs done several ways, potatoes hashed, chipped, and diced, honey, syrup, rolls, and so on, enough to feed a rugby team. It was a most impressive feast at which the Russians did not attend, though invited. They came in after the Yanks had left, and cleared up like vultures.

Meanwhile after politely asking permission the Carney had circled us closely while a photographer in the inflatable filmed the two ships for military publicity. "To show our citizens what work we do out here in dangerous pirate waters." Ted Burke corresponded with them subsequently by email and learned that the Carney had been awarded another badge for an excellent tour of duty.

This whole performance lasted three hours, and convinced us we were indeed free.

At 1900 that night we entered Salalah harbour, tied up to the quay, connected shore power, and left the ship in the capable hands of a Dutch crew including a cook, and Joe Benneton who had successfully delivered Svitzer Busse to Singapore. We were whisked off to the Hilton Hotel, for a welcome shower, and dressed in new clothes generously provided by our Dutch boss, had a few beers, a grand dinner and bed.

21st March, Friday.

Taken to a medical clinic where I discovered I had lost three quarters of a stone, which accounted for the new trousers bought to Barbara's specification being slack like a clown's. My blood pressure was just right and everything else just fine except for the possibility of brucellosis from drinking untreated camels' milk.

Back at the Hilton we had lengthy debriefing conducted by British and American naval officers, and a leader of the expert negotiating team employed by the owners, who were also represented, as well as a manager from our Dutch office. I handed him a roll of incriminating emails concerning the owners' flagrant disregard of our welfare in not providing us with a cook. We would not forget, but then as Ted and I were flown to Dubai to spend a few days in a luxury hotel with our wives, at owners' expense, I was in a forgiving mood.

We had several days in Dubai adjusting to the fact that we had survived, and shedding the worry and responsibility. One day by the pool with a cold beer in hand I assured my wife that I would now retire from the sea, accept no more commissions, no more trips. She smiled and said my English agent had a nice little job for me, just Liverpool to Gibraltar. Well, there couldn't be much harm in that could there?

20:Final trips, Gibraltar and elsewhere.

Barbara and I arrived home from Dubai on 26th March and spent some time visiting relations and friends and generally relaxing and enjoying freedom.

Then on 28th April I went up to Liverpool and took an old tug, "Wellington," to Gibraltar where Barbara joined me for a week's holiday there and in Spain. Then Redwise offered me another safe job, from Pasajes in the Basque part of Spain to Saint Maartens in the Caribbean, where Barbara again joined me for a week's holiday.

While there the Boss 'phoned me from Holland to ask a special favour. It seemed a vessel needed bringing from the Black Sea to Holland and none of his other captains were available. She had completed a two year contract laying the foundations of breakwaters in Georgia, and been damaged when the Russians bombed the port of Poti, but had scrambled away to Constanta in Roumania where I joined her. Her official title was "stone dumper." Originally a tugboat she had been cut in half and a long hold or hopper inserted between the bow with bridge and stern containing the engines. This hopper had large steel doors which were closed when alongside loading boulders and opened when in the position of an intended breakwater. The whole cargo of stone fell through the bottom in seconds which caused this ungainly contraption to leap about alarmingly. However she had now been retired and my job was to return her to owners in Dordrecht, for them to decide whether to scrap her or patch her up for more work. For crew I had an English A.B. a Dutch girl as Mate, and three Russians. The passage through the Dardanelles and to Malta went well and there we took fuel, fresh food, and enjoyed the usual crew bonding. All continued well until past Gibraltar after which the Atlantic swell exposed the unsuitability of this hermaphrodite craft to go to sea. She twisted and flexed and the bottom doors squealed, and ground and gnashed in agony. The young lady Mate had never seen or heard anything like it and could not sleep. When I took over the watch from her in the Bay of Biscay the forecast for rounding Ushant looked bad, so I took her into Brest where we sheltered for three days before completing the voyage to Holland.

From Dordrecht I went to see the boss and protest that I really was now retired and would go no more a-roving. He smiled and said that was a shame as he had some nice jobs coming up, for example one from Dampier in Western Australia to Madagascar. Madagascar sounded interesting and I have friends in Western Australia, so I agreed to go out a week early, see my friends and then do the job.

21:School teaching in China.

Then, by way of emphasising that I was no longer available for sea I took a job teaching "maritime English" in Zhejiang International Maritime College on the island of Zhushan in China. Zhejiang is the modern way of writing Chekiang, my first command, which seemed propitious. My wife and I were met at Shanghai airport by one of the teachers from the college who drove us to a ferry terminal and eventually to Zhushan and the college. We were the only foreigners in this huge establishment of seven thousand students and staff, who made us extremely welcome. The head of my department was professor Wang Wei Ping, a rare combination of high intelligence and feminine beauty.

With Professor Wang and Francis Drake, another Elizabethan seaman.

We had an apartment in the college and took our meals in the staff canteen. My teaching duties only took up two or three hours per day, so with weekends we had plenty of time to explore the island which we did by bus, and took ferries to adjacent islands. In the three months that we were there we made a couple of visits to Shanghai which I found very different from my last calls there forty years previously, during the Cultural Revolution.

134

When the school closed for a week we went to Beijing and saw all the usual tourist attractions including the Ming Tombs and a part of the Great Wall. Though I don't know the Chinese language, which they call PUTONGHUA, not Mandarin, a word of Portuguese origin, I found my partial knowledge of Japanese/ Chinese characters quite useful at times. My teacher colleagues also confirmed that Wah Sung in that part of China does mean "little monkey" and were amused at how I got the name.

Although my wife and I enjoy Chinese cooking we did get bored with so many cold and bony sea-food dishes, and were happy to find an occasional Szechuen restaurant with spicy meat on offer. Apart from in our accommodation the nearest western style toilet was three miles away, the dis-abled toilet in a MacDonald's. It didn't bother me much but my wife found all the squatting awkward especially as public conveniences did not have locks. When the weather warmed up in May we made frequent trips to a beach for a swim. There was a row of food stalls all competing for our custom and we chose one with a well rounded smiling lady. Subsequently we always used her stall and my wife noticed that though we always had the same snacks and drinks the price seemed to go down every time. She had clearly "adopted" us.

When my three months contract was completed we came home to face retirement. But in 2010 we went to Japan for a three week holiday. For me it was the chance to visit some of the temples, castles, and beauty spots I had not been able to get to as a working seaman. Although we found it very expensive compared to the old days the country and people still charmed me. I could not find Noriko but we did spend a few days at Nagasaki with Atsuko my former Chief Engineer's wife. She had lived a number of years in England but when her husband died she had returned home to see out the last of her days. She had brought her little dog from England and lived near a niece and her husband who were clearly very fond of her.

At last I am a retired Elizabethan seaman, settled in Devon with my books, saxophone and paints. When I depict an oriental theme I sign it with a Chinese "chop" I had made before leaving Zhushan.

The chop reads Wah Sung.

Conclusion & Bibliography

Before my unplanned involvement with Somali pirates I knew very little about their country and history. This ignorance was a disadvantage in dealing with our captors and building up a necessary rapport. We had to rely on common sense, patience, and a traveller's instinct for survival. Fortunately we prevailed and emerged not much damaged by the experience.

Since then Somali piracy has continued and in fact flourished. I've heard young men queue up to be pirates and Bedouin girls are eager to marry them. Highjackings still occur and ransoms increase despite expensive counter measures. In the long term Somalia requires a proper government providing education, health, a stable economy, and law and order.

Personally I have tried to learn more about this troubled country and her intriguing people. The following books have helped:-

Understanding Somalia and Somaliland.
Ioan Lewis. Emeritus Professor of Anthropology at the LSE.

Warriors. Life and death among the Somalis.
Gerald Hanley.

The Pillars of Islam & Iman.
Muhammad bin Jamil Zeno.

Where Soldiers Fear to Tread.
John S. Burnett. Former U.N. relief worker in Somalia.

Kidnapped.
Colin Freeman. Sunday Telegraph Foreign Correspondent held to ransom in a Somali cave for 40 days.